Grammar Plus 3

Roy Kingsbury
Felicity O'Dell
Julie Faitaki

Longman

Contents

1 Question words *Who, Which, What* as subjects

Who goes into the water pink and comes out blue?

Which bird is pink, has long legs and a long neck — a parrot or a flamingo?

A flamingo.

Which bird is pink, has one long leg and has its neck under its wing?

A sleeping flamingo.

What gets bigger when you turn it upside down?

The number 6.

Who goes into the water pink and comes out blue?

An English swimmer on a cold day.

What is long, has lots of legs and a red face?

A tired caterpillar.

Subject questions *Who, Which, What*	
Who's blue when he comes out of the water?	**An English swimmer** (is).
Who's got a pen?	**I** have.
Who's taking us to school.	**Mum** (is).
Who lives in that house?	**Our teacher** (does).
Which bird can speak?	**A parrot** (can).
Which bird sleeps during the day?	**An owl** (does).
What gets bigger when you turn it upside down?	**The number 6** (does).
What made him sick?	**The meat** (did). It was bad.

1 A 'subject question' asks about the subject of the verb and begins with the question words **Who? Which? What?** The verb is in the affirmative form, not the interrogative: **Who saw the film on TV?**

2 When we answer a subject question, we often repeat the modal verb or helping verb (**can, do, did, have,** etc.), but we can leave it out.

1 *Fill in the correct question word* Who, Which *or* What *and complete the short answers.*

1 ...Which... bird covers its head when it sleeps?   A flamingo ...does... .

2 .... gets smaller when you turn it upside down?   The number 9 ....

3 .... bird can sleep on one leg?   A flamingo ....

4 .... changes colour when he goes into the water?   An English

swimmer ....

5 .... magazine asked these questions?   *FUN Magazine* ....

2 *Match the questions and the answers.*

1 Who's going on holiday?   a The gardener has.

2 Which student works the hardest in the class?   b I am.

3 Who's taking the children to the circus?   c Liz did.

4 What's red, white and blue?   d Jason does.

5 Who's watered the garden?   e Mum is.

6 Who ironed Jane's skirt for her?   f The British flag is.

1 ..b..   2 ......   3 ......   4 ......   5 ......   6 ......

3 *Look at the answers. Then write the questions using* Which, Who *or* What.

1 ..... / go / to London with you?

Who went to London with you?   Mary did.

2 ..... / be / green / with big eyes and a big mouth?

....   A frog is.

3 ..... / school basketball team / play / the best?

....   Our team does.

4 ..... / boy / can / come to town with me?

....   Jim can.

5 ..... / make / you sick / last night?

....   The fish did.

6 ..... / see / this film?

....   Jane has.

Subject questions	Object questions
Who loves Marian? **James (does).** James loves Marian.	**Who does** Marian **love**? She loves **George**.
Which dog **wants** more food? **The black one (does).**	**Which** apple **do you want**? I want **the red one**.
What made Dad sick? **The chocolate cake (did).**	**What did** Dad **make**? He made **a garden table**.

1 An 'object question' asks about the object of the verb and can also begin with the question words **Who? Which? What?** This time, the verb is in the interrogative form: **Who did you see in town?**

2 The interrogative form of the verb is used for all other question types except subject questions: **Where are you going? When did they arrive? How much did you pay for that CD?**

4 *Make questions using* Who, What *or* Which. *The underlined word is the answer.*

1 Who saw Helen at the cinema yesterday ....?
John saw Helen at the cinema yesterday.

2 Who did John see at the cinema yesterday ....?
John saw Helen at the cinema yesterday.

3 ....?
Mum bought some fresh strawberries yesterday.

4 ....?

    <u>Mum</u> bought some fresh strawberries yesterday.

5 ....?

    <u>Dad</u> brought a friend home last week.

6 ....?

    Dad brought <u>a friend</u> home last week.

5 *Make questions. The words in bold are the answers.*

1 <u>Who flew to Liverpool last week</u>?   **Dad** flew to Liverpool last week.

2 ....?   The dog is eating **his dinner**.

3 ....?   Dad has put on **his grey suit** today.

4 ....?   She's going to visit **her friends**.

5 ....?   **Mother** left early this morning.

6 ....?   George likes **his yellow T-shirt**.

7 ....?   **My friend Paul** wants to live in London.

8 ....?   They met **the new teacher** yesterday.

6 **About you**

The famous rock group 'Pink Frogs' are in Athens for a TV show. You're interviewing the group for the school newspaper. Here are their answers. Write your questions with Who, What, Which, When, How many, *etc. The answers should be the words in bold letters.*

1 <u>Who met you at the airport</u>?   **The TV producer** met us at the airport.

2 ....?   We're staying **for a week**.

3 ....?   We started singing **ten years ago**.

4 ....?   We've made **six records**.

5 ....?   Well, I think **our best CD** is 'High Jump'.

6 ....?   **We** wrote the songs on that collection.

7 ....?   We generally listen to **rock music**.

8 ....?   We go on tour **twice a year**.

2 Relative pronouns *who*, *which*, *that*

Strange but true!

This week FUN Magazine brings you some strange facts.

❗ People who live in large cities walk faster than people who live in the country!

❗ A boy in the USA, who was only thirteen years old, was employed by his school to teach his teachers about computers!

❗ In New York there is a telephone gardener who you can ring and who will talk to your plants!

❗ In the USA there is a magazine which is called *Chocolate News*. It has a brown cover which smells of chocolate!

❗ The largest iceberg which scientists were able to measure was bigger than Belgium!

❗ There are some fish which suffer from seasickness!

Relative pronouns *who* for people	*which* for things and animals
Subject An astronaut is a person **who** goes into space. Artists are people **who** paint pictures.	**Subject** An ant is an insect **which** works hard. There are fish **which** suffer from seasickness.
Object That's the girl **(who(m))** I saw yesterday. Those are the boys **(who(m))** we met.	**Object** That's the bike **(which)** I'd really like. Those are the animals **(which)** I saw at the zoo.

1 When they refer or 'relate' back to people or things in a previous clause, the words **who** and **which** are called relative pronouns.
2 **who** is used for a person or people, **which** for animals and things.
3 The object form **whom** is not often used: we usually use the **who** form instead.
4 We often leave out object relative pronouns in speaking and writing: **That's the girl I saw yesterday. / It's the book I'd like.**

1 *Correct these statements about the text.*

1 People who live in the country walk faster than people who live in cities.

   Wrong. People who live in cities walk faster than people who live in
   the country.

2 An American boy, who was only fifteen years old, taught his teachers
   about computers.

   ....

   ....

3 In New York you can telephone a vet who will talk to your dog.

   ....

4 In the USA there is a magazine with a cover which smells of hamburgers.

   ....

5 There are some fish which suffer from flu.

   ....

2 *Write these nouns in the* who *column or the* which *column.*

bee ✔ gardener ✔
computer   iceberg
astronaut   magazine
teacher   fish
artist   ant
telephone   plant

who	which
gardener	bee

3 *All of these are true, too! Complete the sentences with* who *or* which.

1 Shoes .which. are worn on the right foot wear out faster than left shoes.

2 Sting, ... is now a famous pop star, was once a teacher.

3 There are waiting-rooms at Beijing Railway Station .... can hold
   14,000 people.

4 There is a famous English footballer .... plays for Italy.

5 In the USA you can buy toothpaste for dogs .... tastes of meat.

Who was the English king that had six wives?

I know. Henry the Eighth. He had two wives that he executed and he had two that he divorced.

What happened to the other two wives he had?

I don't know. I saw a film about his life last night but I fell asleep before the end!

Relative pronouns *that* for people	*that* for things and animals
Subject An astronaut is a person **that** goes into space. Artists are people **that** paint pictures.	**Subject** An ant is an insect **that** works hard. There are fish **that** suffer from seasickness.
Object That's the girl (**that**) I saw yesterday. Those are the boys (**that**) we met.	**Object** That's the bike (**that**) I'd really like. Those are the animals (**that**) I saw at the zoo.

1 The relative pronoun **that** can be used for people, animals and things in the singular and plural (in place of **who** or **which**).

2 When the relative pronoun **that** is not the subject of the relative clause, we can leave it out: **That's the girl I saw yesterday.**
BUT when the relative pronoun **who, which, that** is the subject of the following verb, it cannot be left out: **An ant is an insect which / that works hard.**

4 *Match a sentence on the left with a sentence on the right.*
Then join them using relative pronouns.

A platypus is a strange animal.   He discovered America.

Henry the Eighth was a famous king.   They make honey.

Columbus was an explorer.   It lives in Australia.

A computer is a machine.   It can do difficult calculations.

Bees are insects.   He had six wives.

A platypus is a strange animal which / that lives in Australia.

....

....

....

....

5 *Write each of these sentences in two other possible ways, using either a different relative pronoun or missing out the relative pronoun.*

1 Is this the book that you'd like?

   Is this the book which you'd like? / Is this the book you'd like? ....

2 This is the book which I want. ....

   ....

3 Can I read the letter which Ann wrote? ....

   ....

4 You can read all the letters that I got today. ....

   ....

5 What's the name of the family who you met yesterday? ....

   ....

6 *Can we leave out the relative pronouns in these sentences? If so, put a line through them.*

1 **a** Liz is a girl who likes football.   **b** Liz is a girl ~~who~~ other children like.

2 **a** Bees are creatures that scientists often study.   **b** Bees are insects which sting.

3 **a** Mike is a boy who works hard.   **b** Mike is a boy whom teachers like.

4 **a** Ducks are birds that can swim.   **b** Ducks are birds that people eat.

5 **a** This is the pen which John bought.   **b** This is the pen that writes best.

7 About you

Continue these sentences about yourself. Use relative pronouns.

We live in a house *which is very old.* ....

The house is in a street ....

We live in a town ....

I have a friend ....

and I have some other friends ....

I like TV programmes ....

but I don't like programmes ....

3 Definite article *the* and indefinite article *a / an*

We never learn about the USA

MIKE: We have geography twice a week, and I hate it.

LIZ: Why?

MIKE: Well, we never learn about the USA or South America or the Pacific.

LIZ: But you read about places that are very different from our own country and which are a long way away.

MIKE: No, we don't. We're still studying the British Isles.

LIZ: Which places interest you then?

MIKE: Places like the Amazon or the Antarctic. Or China and Japan.

LIZ: Well, your class studied the Far East in geography last month. You were away ill!

Places without *the*	Places with *the*
Continents: Europe, Africa, North and South America, Asia, Australia	**Geographical regions:** the Far East, the Balkans, the Antarctic, the South Pole
Countries: England, Greece, Brazil	**Some countries:** the Netherlands, the USA
Islands: Crete, Rhodes, Malta, Easter Island	**Groups of islands:** the British Isles, the Bahamas, the Ionian Islands, the Hawaiian Islands
Lakes: Lake Como, Lake Erie, Lake Ontario	**Oceans, seas, rivers:** the Pacific, the Dead Sea, the Mediterranean, the Nile, the (River) Thames
Mountains: (Mount) Everest, (Mount) Fuji	**Mountain ranges:** the Alps, the Himalayas, the Rockies, the Andes

1 *Read the text again and correct these sentences.*

1 The children have geography three times a week.
   Wrong. They have geography twice a week.
   ....

2 They often learn about the USA, South America and the Pacific.
   ....
   ....

3 They have finished studying the British Isles.
   ....
   ....

4 Places like the British Isles interest Mike a lot.
   ....
   ....

5 Mike's class studied the Middle East last month.
   ....
   ....

2 ***Add** the or a where necessary or put a '—' where we do not use it*

You probably know that (1) .....the..... Nile is the longest river and that (2) .... Everest in (3) .... Himalayas is the highest mountain in the world. You might even know that (4) .... Lake Erie is in (5) .... North America or that (6) .... Dead Sea is so salty that no fish can live in it. But who was the first man to reach (7) .... South Pole? It was Roald Amundsen, (8) .... Norwegian, who reached the South Pole on 14th December 1911. Robert Scott arrived there a month later and never came back home to (9) .... England. He died on the journey back to base camp.

> That cat's asleep again!
>
> Of course, silly. Cats sleep twelve hours a day.

Indefinite article *a / an* with

Frequency	Measurements	Duration
once **a day**	20 miles **an hour**	12 hours **a day**
twice **a week**	100 kilometres **an hour**	10 minutes **a day**
three times **a month**	50 pence **a kilo**	9 months **a year**
four times **a year**	70 pence **a bottle**	

3 ***Answer the questions in complete sentences.***

1 How fast is this woman driving? (95 km / hour)
   She is driving at 95 kilometres an hour.

2 How much does bread cost? (30 pence / kilo)
   ....

3 How often does Susan brush her teeth? (twice / day)
   ....

4 How many days a week do shops open? (6 days / week)
   ....

5 How long does he exercise? (15 minutes / day)
   ....

6 How often do they go on holiday? (3 times / year)
   ....

In English we use the indefinite article **a / an** with expressions of frequency, measurement and duration, *not* the definite article as in some languages.

4 used to, didn't use to, never used to

I used to have a toy shark

JOHN: When I was a baby I used to have a toy shark.

LIZ: And I used to play with a toy train. I didn't use to play with dolls and I never used to like teddy bears. But I loved my train. I never play with it now, of course.

JANE: I used to play with snails. I used to have a snail that went very slowly. Did you use to have any pets, Jason?

JASON: Yes, I did. I used to have two beetles which lived in a matchbox. But one day I left them in their box on Mum's bed and they escaped. I couldn't find them and Mum was very annoyed.

JOHN: My Mum often used to get annoyed with me too. She used to say 'You'll drive me mad, John!'

You used to drive me mad, too! Actually, you still drive me mad!

Affirmative	Negative	
	Full form	**Short form**
I used to sing	I did not use to sing	I didn't use to sing
you used to sing	you did not use to sing	you didn't use to sing
he used to sing	he never used to sing	he didn't use to sing
we used to sing etc.	we never used to sing etc.	we didn't use to sing etc.

1 We can use **used to + infinitive** to express regular past habits or past states.
2 We can use one of two different negative forms: **I didn't use to sing** or **I never used to sing.**

1 *Complete this paragraph about the children when they were younger. Use* used to, didn't use to *or* never used to *and an appropriate verb.*

When John was a baby he (1) <u>used to have</u> a toy shark and Liz

(2) .... with a toy train. She (3) .... with dolls and

she (4) .... teddy bears. Jane and Jason both (5) ....

pets; Jane had a snail and Jason (6) .... two beetles.

2 *Dad is telling the children about Gran. Fill in the blanks in the sentences with* used to, didn't use to *or* never used to *and the appropriate verb.*
✔ = used to; ✗ = never used to / didn't use to.

1 Gran always spends her holidays abroad now. When she was a child she

<u>never used to spend</u> her holidays abroad. (✗)

2 Gran drives a car now. When she was a child, she ....

a bike. (✔)

3 Gran watches a lot of television now. When she was a child, she ....

.... television — there wasn't any television then! (✗)

She .... to the radio. (✔)

4 Gran likes vegetables now. When she was a child, she ....

vegetables. (✗)

5 Gran and her friends play golf now. When they were younger, they ....

.... golf. (✗) They .... football. (✔)

Interrogative	Short answers	
	Affirmative	**Negative**
Did you use to live in our street?	Yes, I did.	No, I didn't.
Did she ever use to go to a disco?	Yes, she did.	No, she didn't.

3 *Look at Mum's notes about the children as babies. Make questions and then answer them with short answers.*

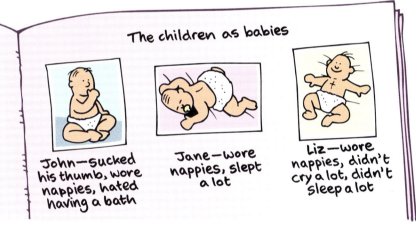

The children as babies

John—sucked his thumb, wore nappies, hated having a bath

Jane—wore nappies, slept a lot

Liz—wore nappies, didn't cry a lot, didn't sleep a lot

1 Did John use to suck his thumb? Yes, he did, but he doesn't now.
....

2 ....

3 ....

4 ....

5 ....

4 *On a separate piece of paper write questions with* used to *to ask a friend. Then ask and answer your questions in pairs.*

Did you use to suck your thumb when you were a baby?
....

Did you use to like green vegetables when you were younger?
....

FUN Magazine

Everybody's wearing *Speedy* trainers

Everyone's wearing **Speedy** trainers. At school, at the disco, everywhere.
Nobody used to wear **Speedy** trainers. **Speedy** trainers are new.
Speedy trainers are the latest fashion in London. Are they fashionable
  anywhere else?
Yes, they'll soon be fashionable everywhere.
Someone starts wearing them in your school. Then everybody wants
  Speedy trainers.
Are YOU still wearing your old trainers? Then you know nothing about fashion.
  No one wants old trainers now.
Join the trend. Buy some **Speedy** trainers.
Put on your **Speedy** trainers and go somewhere special.

Speedy trainers

some	any	no	every
I can hear **somebody**.	Do you know **anybody** here?	**Nobody** used to wear trainers.	Now **everybody**'s wearing trainers.
There is **someone** in the garden.	I don't know **anyone** here.	**No one** knows about her family.	Have you met **everyone** yet?
I can see **something** in the garden.	Have you got **anything** in your bag?	There is **nothing** in my pocket.	Jack knows **everything** about stamps.
My glasses must be **somewhere**.	Is there a post office **anywhere** near here?	There is **nowhere** better in the town.	They'll soon be fashionable **everywhere**.

1 *Ask and answer these questions about the text and write in the answers.*
Use words like something, anybody, everywhere, no one, *etc.*

1 Who's wearing *Speedy* trainers at school now?   *Everybody / Everyone.*

2 Who used to wear *Speedy* trainers at school?   ....

3 Where will *Speedy* trainers soon be fashionable?   ....

4 Who will start wearing them in your school?   ....

5 Then who will want them?   ....

6 If you are still wearing old trainers, what do you
know about fashion? ....

7 Who wants old trainers now? ....

8 Where must you go in your *Speedy* trainers? ....

2 *Complete the sentences with* someone, somebody,
something *or* somewhere. *Use each word at least twice.*

1 I know ..someone........... who has met Kevin Costner.

2 Could you get me .... from the baker's?

3 Will .... help me?

4 I'm sure we've met .... before.

5 Do you know .... called John Brown?

6 I learnt .... very interesting today.

7 I'd like to go .... else now.

8 I met .... yesterday who knows you.

9 They took me .... that was very interesting.

10 I must tell you .... about Mrs Smith.

3 *Match the phrases on the left with phrases on the right to make sentences.*

Liz knows   everywhere she goes.

Jane makes friends   everywhere in Europe

Mum and Dad have met   everyone who lives in the street.

John could eat   everybody in the sports club.

My Dad has been   everyone I met on holiday.

I'm going to write to   everything that there is on the menu.

Liz knows everyone who lives in the street.
....

....

....

....

....

....

some, any, no, every compounds (+ else) + relative pronouns	
People	**Things**
I know **someone who / that** can help.	I've got **something which / that** will interest you.
Do you know **anyone who / that** lives in Paris?	He has told me **everything which / that** his uncle told him.
Everyone who / that knows him likes him.	Have you got **anything which / that** you would like to sell?
There is **no one else who / that** knows this, so don't tell anyone.	Have you **got anything else which / that** Gran would like?

4 *Fill in the gaps with* someone, somebody *or* something *and a relative pronoun.*

1 My Dad knows ....*somebody / someone who / that*.... speaks Japanese.

2 Liz has just found .... she lost last year.

3 Jane is writing to .... lives in Greece.

4 Mike met .... used to live next door to the Bakers.

5 John bought .... Gran liked.

6 Mog ate .... he took from the table.

7 I spoke to .... went to school with Mrs Baker.

8 Jane lost .... belonged to John.

5 *Change **any-** words to **no-** words and vice versa. Make any other changes which are necessary.*

1 There's no one here.   There isn't anyone here.

2 I can't see anything wrong in your composition.   I can see nothing wrong in your composition.

3 We've been nowhere interesting recently.   ....

4 Liz doesn't know anything about world history.   ....

5 There's nobody here who speaks Chinese.   ....

6 *Complete the sentences. Use **anything else, anywhere else, somewhere else, no one else, something else.***

1 The book Liz wanted for Gran isn't in that book shop. She must look

   somewhere else .

2 I've told you all I know. I don't know ....

3 Jane thinks she has bought everything that she needs for the cake.

   But I'm sure she needs ....

4 Liz told Jane her secret but .... knows.

5 Did the Bakers only go to France for their holidays last year or did

   they go .... as well?

7 **About you**

Read this paragraph which Jane wrote. Then complete the paragraph about yourself.

I like everyone who is friendly but I don't like anyone who hurts animals. I like studying everything which Miss Wall teaches but I don't like anything at school which is too difficult for me. I would like to live somewhere in the country but I wouldn't like to live anywhere that is far from the sea.

I like everyone ....

but I don't like anyone ....

I like studying everything ....

but I don't like anything at school ....

I would like to live somewhere ....

and / but I wouldn't like to live anywhere that is ....

6 should and ought to

FUN Magazine

Lisa Young answers your questions

Your parents should listen to you

Dear John,

Thank you for your letter. So you want to go somewhere in the evenings but your parents want you to stay at home. This is quite a common problem.

Of course you ought to listen to your parents. They're right. You should work hard at school. No one should go out every evening and you shouldn't come home late at night — you're still young.

But you're right too. Everyone ought to spend time with their friends. We all need some freedom.

You should talk to your parents. Promise them that you will do your homework first. Then you should be able to spend some time with your friends.

Good luck!

Lisa

Affirmative	Negative	
	Full form	**Short form**
I should wait you should wait he should wait etc.	I should not wait you should not wait he should not wait etc.	I shouldn't wait you shouldn't wait he shouldn't wait etc.
I ought to wait you ought to wait	(I ought not to wait) (you ought not to wait)	(I oughtn't to wait) (you oughtn't to wait)

1 We use the modal verbs **should** or **ought to** to express an obligation.
2 Although the negative forms **ought not to** and **oughtn't to** are grammatically correct, they both sound very formal, and nowadays people usually use **shouldn't**.

1 *Read Lisa Young's letter again and correct these statements.*

1 John shouldn't listen to his parents. *Wrong. He should listen to his parents.*

2 John ought to work hard at home. ....

3 Everyone should go out every evening. ....

4 John should come home late in the evening.

....

5 John shouldn't spend time with his friends.

....

2 *Change* should *to* ought to *and vice versa.*

1 Jane should help Mum and John ought to help Dad.
   Jane ought to help Mum and John should help Dad.

2 Liz ought to clean her shoes and Mike should wash his hands.

   ....

3 Mum should do the ironing and Dad ought to clean the kitchen.

   ....

4 All children should learn a foreign language.

   ....

5 You ought to help me with *my* homework, and I should help you with yours.

   ....

6 You should listen to your parents and they ought to listen to you.

   ....

Interrogative	Short answers	
	Affirmative	Negative
should I wait?	Yes, I should.	No, I shouldn't.
should you wait?	Yes, you should.	No, you shouldn't.
should he wait?	Yes, he should.	No, he shouldn't
etc.	etc.	etc.

People rarely use **ought to** in questions nowadays.

3 *Make questions using the words provided, then write short answers.*

1 If you / cut / your knee, / should / wash it?
   If you cut your knee, should you wash it? Yes, you should.

2 If the children / break / window, / should / tell Dad?

   ....

3 If Jane / have / important exam, / should / go out every night?

   ....

4 If I / have / problem, / should / write to Lisa Young?

   ....

5 If the Bakers / go / on holiday, / should / take Scamp with them?

   ....

7 Present perfect simple and past simple

What have you done today?

It's Saturday afternoon.
Peter, a neighbour, is talking to Dad.

PETER: You look very busy, Jim. What have you done today?

JIM: I've done a few jobs. So far I've cleaned the car. And I've mended Jane's bike.

PETER: Well, you've done a lot. And it's only half past three. But you don't look very happy.

JIM: Well, I haven't done anything that I really wanted to!

PETER: What did you really want to do?

JIM: I really wanted to have a game of golf.

Present perfect simple with *today*, *this week*, *this month*, *this year*

Today I have cleaned my car and mended Jane's bike.
This week it has rained three times.
She has eaten a pizza and two hamburgers **so far this evening**.
This month you have had two accidents on your bike.
This year they have won the lottery three times!
They haven't been to London **this month**.

---

1 One use of the present perfect simple is to describe an action or actions which has/have happened within a period of time which is still going on, for example **today**, **this week**, etc.:

this week

| Last Sat. | 1 | 2 | 3 | Now | Next Sat. |

It has already rained three times this week.

2 The time phrase (**this year**, **today**, etc.) can go at the beginning or at the end of the sentence: [**This year**] **they have won the lottery three times** [**this year**].

---

1 *Read the text again, then ask and answer these questions.*

1 What day is it? It's Saturday.

2 What has Dad done today? ....

3 What has Dad cleaned, his car or his room? ....

4 What else has he done today? ....

5 Why doesn't he look very happy? ....

I hate school! Tests! Tests! Nothing but tests! We had four last week and so far we've had two this week.

Present perfect simple with *today, this week, this month*, etc.	Past simple with *yesterday, last week, last month*, etc.
Jane **has had** a test **today**.	Jane **had** a test **yesterday**, too.
It **has rained** three times **this month**.	It only **rained** once **last month**.
How many books **have you read this year**?	How many books **did you read last year**?
Jane **has had** a test **this morning**.	She **had** a test **this morning**.
(It's still morning.)	(It's afternoon or evening now.)

1 We use the present perfect simple with a period of time which has not yet ended: **I've done a lot of jobs this morning.** (It's 11 o'clock.)

2 We use the simple past with a period of time which finished in the past (**last year, yesterday**, etc.) — even **this morning** when we are talking in the evening: **We went to town this morning.** (It's now 20.00.)

2 *Fill in the blanks with the present perfect simple or the past simple of the verbs given.*

1 They .... *bought* .... (buy) a new car last year.

2 We .... (not have) any English tests so far this week.

3 It .... (not snow) much this year but it .... (snow) a lot last year.

4 They .... (not play) golf today but they .... (play) tennis yesterday.

5 She .... (be) to the cinema twice this month.

6 He .... (beat) everyone in the tennis club last Sunday.

7 My friend .... (buy) two CDs so far this week.

8 Her mother .... (give) her four CDs last week.

8 The passive: *has(n't) / have(n't) been done, will / won't be done*

Here is the news

This is Radio Four and here is the 8 o'clock news for today, Friday the fourteenth of February.

£1,000,000 has been stolen from the England Bank in London. No one was injured but three people who were suffering from shock have been taken to hospital. Three men have already been arrested.

Many villages in the north of Scotland have been cut off by severe snowstorms. The main road to the north has been blocked since six o'clock last night. It has not been possible to clear the road because snow is still falling.

England has been beaten by Greece in the Europe Cup match. Now Greece will go forward to the final. The English Captain has not yet spoken to the press about the result.

Affirmative		Negative	
Full form	**Short form**	**Full form**	**Short form**
I have been injured	I've been injured	I have not been injured	I haven't been injured
you have been injured	you've been injured	you have not been injured	you haven't been injured
he has been injured	he's been injured	he has not been injured	he hasn't been injured
etc.	etc.	etc.	etc.

1 *Read the text again and then fill in the blanks in these news reports.*

1 £1,000,000 .....has been stolen.. from the England Bank. Three people ....
.... to hospital. Three men .... by the police.

2 Many villages in the north of Scotland .... by severe
snowstorms. The main road to the north .... since six
o'clock last night. It .... possible to clear the road
because snow is still falling.

3 The English team .... by Greece. The English Captain

.... to the press yet.

2 *Complete the sentences with* **has been** *or* **have been.**

1 Her grandfather .....*has been*...... taken to hospital.

2 Lots of umbrellas .... left on the bus today.

3 This present .... made by the children.

4 Many people .... injured in football matches this year.

5 Nothing .... stolen from the post office this year.

6 All flights this morning .... cancelled because of the storms.

7 The lottery .... not .... won by anybody this week.

8 They .... chosen to play for the school football team.

Interrogative	Short answers	
	Affirmative	**Negative**
have you been seen?	Yes, I have.	No, I haven't.
has he been seen?	Yes, he has.	No, he hasn't.
have they been seen?	Yes, they have.	No, they haven't.
etc.	etc.	etc.

3 *Make questions. Choose the best verb from the box. Use the present perfect passive form. Complete the short answer to the question.*

| repair   block   paint   ~~send~~   steal   wash |

1 .....*Has*.... the letter already ......*been sent*....... to London? Yes, ...*it has*... .

2 Look in your bag. .... your purse .... ?

Yes, ...

3 .... these pictures really .... by the youngest child

in the school? Yes, ...

4 .... the car .... yet? No, ...

5 .... these clothes .... yet? No, ...

6 .... all the roads .... by snow? Yes, ...

Affirmative		Negative	
Full form	**Short form**	**Full form**	**Short form**
I will be met	I'll be met	I will not be met	I won't be met
you will be met	you'll be met	you will not be met	you won't be met
he will be met	he'll be met	he will not be met	he won't be met
etc.	etc.	etc.	etc.
Interrogative		**Short answers**	
Will it be done this week?		Yes, it will.	No, it won't.

4 **Make sentences about Liz and John and their bikes. Put the words in the correct order.**

1 has   yet   not   repaired   been   Liz's bike
   Liz's bike has not been repaired yet.
   ....

2 this afternoon   will   repaired   Liz's bike   be
   ....

3 John's bike   be   this afternoon   done   won't
   ....

4 It   finished   before Saturday   won't   be
   ....

5 probably   It   finished   be   will   on Saturday afternoon
   ....

6 will both   The bikes   mended   by Sunday   be
   ....

5 *Dad is making a number of telephone calls. He wants to find out if some jobs have been done. Write answers to his questions.*

1 DAD: Has the car been repaired yet?

GARAGE (✔, Thursday): *Yes, it has. It was repaired on Thursday.*

2 DAD: Have my daughter's shoes been mended yet?

SHOEMAKER (✗, next Wednesday): ....

....

3 DAD: Has my bookcase been built yet?

CARPENTER (✔, Monday): ....

....

4 DAD: Has our washing-machine been repaired yet?

ELECTRICIAN (✗, next week): ....

....

6 *Read this newspaper article. Make questions about the article using the words provided. Write full answers to your questions.*

Runaway Boy Has Not Been Found

A teenage boy has run away from home for the fifth time. He was last seen on a flight to Manila. His documents were checked at Heathrow Airport but no one noticed that he was using his father's passport. His father's credit cards have also been taken. If the cards are used, the police will be told and the boy will be found. He will be brought home immediately. Will he be punished? His father says 'No, he won't. We will just be happy to have him safe at home again.'

1 When / boy / last / seen?

When was the boy last seen?
The boy was last seen on a
flight to Manila.

2 documents / checked / Heathrow Airport? ....

....

3 his father's credit cards / taken? ....

....

4 What / happen / if credit cards / used? ....

....

5 Will / boy / punished? ....

....

9 Direct and indirect objects with *give*, *send*, *take*, etc.

Read me the instructions, please

DAD: I can't understand how to use this video camera. Read the instructions to me, Liz.

LIZ: Why have you got a video camera, Dad?

DAD: I want to give Mum one for her birthday. Now, please read me the instructions!

LIZ: Why did you buy her a video camera?

DAD: She can use it when we go on holiday to America. And I want to make her a film of the family for her birthday too. But it's a secret. I promised her a surprise. So don't tell her anything.

LIZ: Of course I won't tell her. Pass me the instructions and I'll read them. Where did you get it from?

DAD: I rang a company and ordered one. They sent me a box with the camera, batteries and everything in it.

LIZ: All right, Dad. Now listen. 'First .... '
Oh no, Mum's coming. She's bringing us some tea. Hide everything. Quickly!

Some verbs with two objects

bring   buy   do   get   give   make   pass   promise   read   send   take   tell

Mum **brought** (Dad) | a cup of tea.

Mum **brought** | a cup of tea | (to Dad.)

She's **given** (him) | a book.

She's **given** | a book | (to him.)

He **made** (the children) | a cake.

He **made** | a cake | (for the children.)

Please **read** (us) | a story.

Please **read** | a story | (to us.)

1 Certain verbs in English take two objects, a direct object and an indirect object (often a person or personal pronoun). With these verbs we can put the indirect object (without a preposition) before the direct object: **Mum brought Dad [= to Dad] a cup of tea.**

2 We can put the direct object before the indirect, but we must then use the preposition **to** or **for**: **Dad gave a video camera <u>to Mum</u>. / She made a cake <u>for the children</u>.**

1 *Rewrite these sentences. Place the indirect object right after the verb.*

1 Liz is going to read the instructions to Dad.
   Liz is going to read Dad the instructions.

2 Dad wants to give a video camera to Mum.

   ....

3 He wants to make a film of the family for her.

   ....

4 Dad had promised a surprise to Mum.

   ....

5 The company sent a box to Dad.

   ....

6 Mum's bringing some tea to them.

   ....

2 *Choose and write the correct object — direct or indirect.*

1 We gave ......*him*...... a book.   (him)/ to him

2 I must get a birthday present ....   my mother / for my mother

3 Our parents promised .... a trip to Australia.   us / to us

4 Will you do .... a favour?   to me / me

5 Will you take the coffee .... ?   to Marian / Marian

6 Pass .... the salt, please.   me / to me

7 Liz sent .... a postcard.   Gran / to Gran

8 Take these books ....   the teacher / to the teacher

3 About you

Use the verbs get, give, bring, make, send, *etc., and write a short paragraph about the presents you received on your last birthday.*

One of my friends sent me ....

....

....

....

....

10 Some verbs and prepositions

Thank you for your letter

Dear Eleni,

Thank you for your letter. Congratulations on your exam results. You waited for the results for a long time, I know, but now you can relax.

We arrived in New York three days ago. We haven't suffered from the long flight, fortunately, and have spent all our time till now sightseeing. I love looking at all the tall buildings here and I also love listening to the New York accent. The people are very friendly. They all smile at you and say 'Have a nice day!' They talk to you much more than English people do. One man even paid for our meal in a restaurant because he liked our accents!

I am thinking of you a lot and am looking forward to your next letter.

Lots of love,
Liz

Some common verbs with their prepositions

arrive at / in	pay for
believe in	read about
belong to	smile at
depend on	suffer from
laugh at	talk to
listen to	think of / about
look at	wait for
look forward to	

apologise to somebody for
congratulate somebody on
thank somebody for

1 These verbs are followed by certain prepositions when they are followed by a noun or a pronoun: **Look at them!**. When there is no following noun or pronoun, we do not use the preposition: **Look! Wait! Listen!**

2 NOTE: **to arrive in** usually means to reach a place or country (**He arrived in Montreal yesterday**). **to arrive at** usually means to reach a small place or event (**We arrived at the party late**).

1 *This is Eleni's reply to Liz. Fill in the prepositions.*

Dear Liz,

Thank you (1) ......_for_...... your letter. I've been waiting (2) .... your news. I'm glad you arrived safely (3) .... New York. What do you think (4) .... the USA? Is it expensive? How much do you have to pay (5) .... a meal in a restaurant?

I'm looking forward (6) .... your next letter.

Love,
Eleni

2 *Match a phrase on the right with a phrase on the left and write it in.*

1 The watch belongs .....to Jane.....   in ghosts.

2 The children are waiting ....   from flu.

3 Jane doesn't believe ....   to Jane. ✔

4 Mum congratulated Liz ....   on the weather.

5 Mrs Baker is suffering ....   for the bus.

6 The success of the picnic depends ....   on her good marks.

3 *Complete the questions with a preposition. Then look at the picture and write the answer.*

1 What is Liz looking .....at..... ?
   Liz is looking at a book.

2 Who is John smiling .... ?

   ....

3 What is Jane reading .... ?

   ....

4 What is Mog thinking .... ?

   ....

5 Who is Mum talking .... ?

   ....

4 **About you**

Complete these sentences about yourself. The first word you write in each case must be a preposition.

1 I love listening ...to my Bon Jovi CDs..

2 I enjoy reading ....

3 I love talking ....

4 I often laugh ....

5 I'm looking forward ....

6 I believe ....

7 When I was last ill I was suffering ....

11 Some adjectives and prepositions

I'm not very fond of school reports!

John's school report was waiting for them when they got back home from America.

REPORT

Pupil's name: John Baker   **Class:** 2B

English	John is very keen on English but he is terrible at spelling.
Mathematics	John is interested in mathematics and he is very good at geometry.
French	I am quite pleased with John's progress this year. He is doing much better at French.
History	John is not very good at history and I was not surprised at his poor mark in the last test.
Geography	I am disappointed with John's work in geography this year. I hope he will work harder at his geography next year.
Sport	John is excellent at football and we are all proud of his performance in the school team.

> **good at something, interested in something, afraid of someone**
>
> He's **awful / bad / terrible / good / excellent**   **at** sport.
> New York is **famous**   **for** its skyscrapers.
> Are you **interested**   **in** history?
> They're **afraid / fond / proud**   **of** their father.
> They aren't very **keen**   **on** football.
> She's usually **nice / polite / rude**   **to** people.
> We're **angry / bored / disappointed / pleased**   **with** our teacher.

1 **Mum is telling Dad about John's school report.**
Fill in the correct prepositions.

❛ John's school report wasn't so bad after all. Of course, he's terrible

(1) ..at.. spelling and he isn't very good (2) .... history, but he's

keen (3) .... English, interested (4) .... mathematics and very good

(5) .... geometry. His geography teacher's disappointed (6) .... him,

but his French teacher's pleased (7) .... his progress this year. He's

excellent (8) .... sport and the school's proud (9) .... his performance

in the school team. So don't be angry (10) .... him. ❜

2 *Say and write questions and answers about these pictures.*

1
Jane / good? – French

What's Jane good at?
She's good at French.

2
John / keen? – music

....
....

3
The Bakers / fond? –
animals

....
....

4
Mog / afraid? – mice

....
....

5
she / bored? – his story

....
....

6
Liz / interested? – art

....
....

3 *Find ten adjectives in this box. You can read across or down.*
Then write them and add their prepositions.

K	A	F	R	A	I	D	E	P	Z
E	I	N	Z	L	N	M	I	O	N
E	E	V	O	I	T	S	I	L	T
N	I	C	E	F	E	B	C	I	E
O	K	D	U	O	R	I	M	T	R
R	F	G	B	O	E	D	K	E	R
U	O	O	O	E	S	M	A	R	I
D	N	O	R	K	T	I	E	O	B
E	D	D	E	O	E	M	C	Y	L
W	V	X	D	H	D	D	G	F	E

1 ....keen........ ....on....

2 ....

3 ....

4 ....

5 ....

6 ....

7 ....

8 ....

9 ....

10 ....

12 Gerunds after prepositions

Famous for winning gold medals

What are you reading?

The Guinness Book of Records, 1995. It's great. It's a book that tells you about all kinds of interesting people and things. Just look at these.

Raymond Clarence Ewry

This American is famous for winning more gold medals in the modern Olympic Games than anyone else. He won them for athletics in 1900, 1904 and 1908.

Milind Deshmukh

This man dreamt of seeing his name in the Guinness Book of Records. So he thought of walking with a milk bottle on his head. At Pune in India in 1993 he succeeded in walking 104.2 kilometres before he dropped the bottle.

Henri Rochatain

This Frenchman was very good at balancing on a tightrope. In 1975 he spent six months on a tightrope in France and was even able to sleep on the tightrope without falling off.

Some adjectives and verbs with their prepositions + gerunds

Adjective + preposition + gerund	Verb + preposition + gerund
He's **famous for winning** medals.	They **believe in working** hard.
She's **fond of skating**.	I **look forward to going** home.
He was **good at balancing**.	He **dreamt of seeing** his name in the book.
She is **proud of being** tidy.	He **thought of walking** with a milk bottle on his head.
They're **afraid of going** to the dentist.	She **succeeded in passing** the exam.
They're **bored with doing** history.	We **paid** Jack **for working** here.

Note that the preposition *without* is followed by the gerund:
You can't make an omelette **without breaking** eggs.

When a verb follows a preposition, it is always in the form of a gerund — or the *-ing* form of the verb: **He's good *at running*.** / **I believe *in working* hard.**

1 *Look at the text again and fill in the blanks in John's letter to Gran. Write a preposition and a gerund.*

Dear Gran,

I've been reading the <u>Guinness Book of Records</u> which you sent me for my birthday. I've learnt some really interesting things! Have you heard of Ewry? He's famous
(1) ..<u>for</u>.. ..<u>winning</u>... more gold medals in the modern Olympic Games than anyone else.

Milind Deshmukh dreamt (2) .... his name in the <u>Guinness Book of Records</u>. So he thought (3) .... as far as he could with a milk bottle on his head. He succeeded (4) .... 104.2 kilometres.

Henri Rochatain was very good (5) .... on a tightrope. He was able to sleep on a tightrope (6) .... off.

2 *Write in the correct prepositions and the gerund of the verb.*

1 I've often thought ...<u>of being</u>.............. (be) an engineer.

2 He succeeded .... (get) the job

3 I'm fond .... (play) football.

4 I've always dreamt .... (go) to Australia.

5 She isn't very good .... (swim).

6 I'm bored .... (read) this book.

7 You can't sit in that café .... (eat) something!

8 My sister's looking forward .... (start) work.

3 **About you**

Complete this paragraph about yourself. Add a preposition and a gerund to complete each sentence.

I'm very good <u>at playing tennis</u>. and I'm also good ....

I'm not very good .... , but I'm excellent ....

I'm interested .... and I'm also keen ....

I believe .... and I look forward ....

13 Tag questions

It's a lovely day, isn't it?

LIZ: It's a lovely day, isn't it? Let's go for a picnic.

JANE: You haven't tidied your room yet, so Mum won't let you go anywhere.

LIZ: You'll help me, won't you? Then we can go somewhere nice.

JOHN: Let's go to the lake on our bikes. We didn't go there at all last year, did we?

LIZ: I don't want to go to the lake. I want to go to the wood. We could climb some trees and we could look for insects, couldn't we?

JANE: I don't like climbing trees now. I fell and hurt myself last time I climbed a tree. I just want to go to the park.

They talk a lot, don't they?

Yes, but they can't decide anything!

Affirmative verb + Negative tag	Negative verb + Affirmative tag
You are fond of him, **aren't you**?	**You aren't** afraid of him, **are you**?
He is learning English, **isn't he**?	**He isn't** learning French, **is he**?
He was rude to them, **wasn't he**?	**She wasn't** nice to me, **was she**?
We were having tea at four, **weren't we**?	**You weren't** listening, **were you**?
They've got a car, **haven't they**?	**They haven't** got a boat, **have they**?
Liz has tidied her room, **hasn't she**?	**Liz hasn't** tidied her desk, **has she**?
You will help me, **won't you**?	**Mum won't** be angry, **will she**?

1 'Tag questions' are questions formed with affirmative and negative statements + question phrases: these phrases (often represented in other languages by one set phrase) are formed in English with the helper verb of the sentence.

2 We use tag questions to ask for information or for confirmation of what has been said.

3 Note the two main forms:
   a Affirmative sentence + negative tag question form. The short form of **not** is combined with the helper verb: **... , isn't she? ... , won't we?**
   b Negative sentence + affirmative tag question form: **... , are you? ... , is he?**

4 The subject of the tag phrase at the end is always a pronoun, and in writing we always use a comma before the tag: *John's right, isn't he?*

1 *Add the tag to these questions.*

1 He isn't very good at history, ... *is he* .... ?

2 Mary's going to the post office, ... ?

3 Mog was looking for something, ... ?

4 You won't do it, ... ?

5 Jim's got two pets, ... ?

6 They weren't angry with me, ... ?

7 Dad will help me, ... ?

8 You haven't broken it, ... ?

9 Jane has taken Scamp for a walk, ... ?

10 That film was good, ... ?

You do, don't you? **You did, didn't you?**	**You don't, do you?** **You didn't, did you?**
You like climbing trees, **don't you**? **John wants** to go out, **doesn't he**? **They went** to the park, **didn't they**? **He has** breakfast at ten, **doesn't he**? **They had** dinner late, **didn't they**?	**They don't** want to go out, **do they**? **Liz doesn't** like insects, **does she**? **They didn't go** to the lake, **did they**? **You don't have** lunch at 12.00, **do you**? **He didn't have** lunch today, **did he**?

When the main sentence does not contain a helper verb (a modal, **has / have, had, is / are / was / were**, etc.) we use **do / does** (for present) or **did** (for simple past): **He doesn't smoke,** *does* **he? / She won,** *didn't* **she?**

2 *This is part of an interview with Linda, a model. Add suitable question tags.*

REPORTER: Linda, you started modelling two years ago, (1) *didn't you* ? And you come from England, (2) .... ?

LINDA: Yes, and I still live with my family here. You didn't know that, (3) .... ?

REPORTER: No, I didn't. Now, you do some fashion shows with your twin sister Monica, (4) .... ?

LINDA: Yes. We model the same dress. People have a pleasant surprise.

REPORTER: She doesn't like modelling much, though, (5) .... ?

LINDA: Unfortunately, no. This new idea's been very popular. We sometimes fight about it but all sisters disagree sometimes, (6) .... ?

You should enter the school painting competition, Jane.

I should, shouldn't I? What shall I paint?

You can paint something about the environment, can't you?

Mmmm! I could paint a picture about pollution, couldn't I? Who knows, I might even win first prize!

Affirmative modal + Negative tag	Negative modal + Affirmative tag
Jane can paint well, **can't she**?	John can't paint, **can he**?
You could help me, **couldn't you**?	You couldn't do it, **could you**?
He would like this, **wouldn't he**?	He wouldn't like that, **would he**?
He should tell her, **shouldn't he**?	You shouldn't smoke, **should you**?
He used to live here, **didn't he**?	Liz didn't use to cry much, **did she**?

3 *Someone added tag questions to the sentences below but made some mistakes. Tick the correct tag questions. Underline and correct the wrong ones.*

1 Mog would love some milk now, wouldn't he? ....✔........

2 We shouldn't make our beaches dirty, <u>would we?</u> *should we?*

3 Tom used to drive a red car, doesn't he? ....

4 You couldn't help me, can you? ....

5 Mary can't drive, can't she? ....

6 We should write on recycled paper, shouldn't we? ....

7 We can go somewhere for an ice-cream, don't we? ....

8 Ann would like a red dress, shouldn't she? ....

there is, *there was*, *there will be*, and some irregular question tags
There is a lot of coke in the fridge, **isn't there**? **There wasn't** much milk in the fridge, **was there**? **There won't be** many people there, **will there**?

I'm right, **aren't I**?	**I'm not** late, **am I**?
I'm doing well in French, **aren't I**?	**I'm not doing** very well at history, **am I**?
Stop that noise, **will you**?	**Let's go** for a swim, **shall we**?

4 *Write in the correct question tags to complete the sentences.*

1 There aren't any eggs left, *are there* ?

2 I'm late, ... ?

3 Liz, take Dad his tea, ... ?

4 There's nothing to do here, ... ?

5 There won't be anybody there now, ... ?

6 I'm not very good at this, ... ?

7 She's doing very well at school, ... ?

8 You used to like meat, ... ?

9 He can't swim, ... ?

10 But you can swim very well, ... ?

5 *Mum and Dad are talking about Liz.*
Add the tag questions to the dialogue.

DAD: There's something wrong with Liz, (1) *isn't there* ? She daydreams a lot and she

hasn't been eating much, (2) .... ? She shouldn't go on a diet at her age.

And she stays home a lot these days, (3) .... ? She isn't worrying about

school, (4) .... ? No, she wouldn't keep something like that a secret.

MUM: You've asked her about it, (5) .... ?

DAD: Of course, I have. I'm her father, (6) .... ? But she didn't tell

me anything.

MUM: A girl doesn't tell her parents things like that, (7) .... ?

DAD: What things? You've known all the time, (8) .... ?

MUM: Don't worry, it's her age. She's in love again — the third time this year!

6 *Match the sentences on the left with their question tags on the right.*

1 She won first prize, ✔   a could he?

2 Jim likes basketball a lot,   b haven't they?

3 It was a good game,   c does he?

4 They've got two brown dogs,   d wasn't it?

5 Tom couldn't fly his kite today,   e didn't she? ✔

6 He doesn't like me,   f doesn't he?

14 Future continuous

My dad'll be helping me

MIKE: When can I phone you to talk about going to the cinema?

LIZ: Well, not this evening.

MIKE: Why not?

LIZ: Well, we'll be eating from about half past seven to eight. Then I'll be watching a programme about China.

MIKE: OK, I won't ring this evening. Anyway, my dad'll be helping me with my homework.

LIZ: What did you want to see?

MIKE: I wanted to see the new Tom Hanks film.

LIZ: Oh, I won't be seeing that at the cinema.

MIKE: Why not?

LIZ: My dad's getting a video copy of it and we'll be watching it at home this weekend.

Affirmative	Negative
Full form / Short form	**Full form / Short form**
I will / I'll be watching	I will not / I won't be watching
you will / you'll be watching	you will not / you won't be watching
he will / he'll be watching	he will not / he won't be watching
etc.	etc.

1 The future continuous is used for an action which will be taking place at a certain time in the future: **This time tomorrow I'll be flying to London**.

2 It is also used for an action which has definitely been planned for the future: **I'll be seeing him tomorrow.**

1 *Ask and answer these questions about the conversation. Write the answers.*

1 Why won't Mike phone Liz at half past seven?

   <u>Because she'll be eating then.</u>..

2 Why won't he phone her at 8.30?

   ....

3 What will Mike's dad be doing this evening?

   ....

4 Where and when will Liz be watching the new Tom Hanks film?

   ....

2 *Liz and John know exactly what they'll be doing this weekend. Make sentences about their arrangements for the weekend.*

1 Saturday morning / she / go swimming

On Saturday morning she'll be going swimming.

2 Saturday afternoon / he / do some shopping

....

3 Saturday evening / they / watch a video

....

4 Sunday morning / she / help Mum

....

5 Sunday afternoon / they / visit Gran

....

Interrogative	Short answers	
	Affirmative	**Negative**
will I be watching?	Yes, I will.	No, I won't.
will you be watching?	Yes, you will.	No, you won't.
will he be watching?	Yes, he will.	No, he won't.
etc.	etc.	etc.

Will you be watching the new Disney film on TV tonight?

No, of course I won't.

Yes, she will.

3 *Look at Mike and Liz's conversation again. Make questions about the conversation and answer them. Write short answers.*

1 Liz / eat / six o'clock?

Will Liz be eating at six o'clock? No, she won't.

2 Liz / watch / programme about China this evening?

....

3 Mike's dad / help him with his homework this evening?

....

4 Liz and Mike / watch the new Tom Hanks film at the cinema together this weekend?

....

5 Liz / watch it / at home with her family this weekend?

....

Future time clauses with *when, after, before, until, as soon as*

When I'm 25, I'll be a famous actress

Monday 1 January

I've been thinking about my future.

I want to be rich and famous when I grow up. I'll be a famous rock star before I am 20. When I'm 25, I'll be a famous actress, and when I'm 30, I'll retire.

But before I do all that, I want to travel around the world. As soon as I leave school, I'll take my rucksack and some money and I'll travel round Europe by train. I'll stay in Europe until I have seen everything that I want to see. After I've seen everything in Europe, I'll go to Australia. When I've seen everything in Australia, I'll go to the USA. I won't leave the USA until I've spent all my money.

And then, when I've seen the world, I'll come home and join a rock group.

Present simple tense in future time clauses	
when	Liz will be an actress **when she is** 25.
after	John will get a job **after he leaves** school.
before	Liz will take some exams **before the term finishes**.
until / till	Please wait here **until / till your parents arrive**.
not until	I won't phone you **until I get** home.
as soon as	Liz'll travel round Europe **as soon as she leaves** school.

We never use the future tense **will do** after the joining words **when, after, before, until / till** and **as soon as.** Even when we are talking about the future, we use the present simple: **I'll see you *when I come* home** (NOT 'when I will come').

1 *Ask and answer these questions about Liz's plans. Write full sentences.*

1 What does Liz want to be when she grows up?
   She wants to be rich and famous when she grows up.

2 When will she be a famous rock star?
   ....

3 When will she be a famous actress?
   ....

4 What will she do before she becomes a star?

....

5 What will she do as soon as she leaves school?

....

> I'll do my homework when I've watched this programme.

> Oh, no, you won't. You can only watch TV after you've finished your homework.

Present perfect tense in future time clauses

when	John will buy a car **when he has passed** his driving test.
after	John will leave school **after he has taken** his exams.
before	Mum will get home **before Dad has finished** work.
until / till	Liz will stay in the USA **until / till she's spent** all her money.
not until	Don't go **until you have thanked** Jill for your present.
as soon as	Give me back the money **as soon as you've sold** your bike.

We never use the future perfect tense **will have done** after the joining words **when, after, before, until / till** and **as soon as**. We use the present perfect simple: **I'll stay here *until I have finished* my work** (NOT ~~until I will have finished~~').

2 *Ask and answer some more questions about Liz's plans. Write full sentences.*

1 How long will Liz stay in Europe?

   She will stay in Europe until she has seen everything.

2 How long will she stay in Australia?

....

3 When will she leave the USA?

....

4 When will she come home and join a rock group?

....

LIZ: What are you doing tomorrow when you go on your class excursion?

JANE: As soon as everyone arrives at school, we're going to the Houses of Parliament by bus.

LIZ: If I ask your teacher, could I come too?

JANE: Of course, but if you come, I'm staying at home!

Present simple and present perfect in future time clauses

when	I'm going to buy a computer **when I've saved** enough money.
after	John is meeting a friend **after school finishes** today.
until / till	The bus won't go **until / till everyone has arrived**.

3 *Complete the sentences. Put the verb in brackets in the correct form — present simple or present perfect.*

1 John will have a surprise as soon as he .....*gets*.... home, won't he? (get)

2 Liz will watch some TV after she .... her homework, won't she? (finish)

3 Dad won't give Liz her pocket money until she .... for being so rude, will he? (apologise).

4 Mum and Dad will leave the restaurant when they .... for their meal, won't they? (pay)

5 Mike will thank his aunt for the present when he .... to her next weekend, won't he? (write)

4 *First put the words in the right order and write the questions.*

1 you / do you / to do / when / grow up / want
   What .....*do you want to do when you grow up*..................... ?

2 you / will you / as soon as / today / school / leave / do
   What .... ?

3 tonight / before / you / go to bed / are you going / to do

What .... ?

4 after / wake up / will you do / tomorrow morning / you

What .... ?

Now write true answers to the questions you have written.

5 When I grow up I want to be a doctor. ....

6 ....

7 ....

8 ....

5 **_Look at the pictures and complete the sentences._**

1 You shouldn't start cooking until you have washed your hands. ....

2 You mustn't cross the road until the cars ....

3 You mustn't post your letter until you ....

4 You mustn't go to bed until you ....

5 You shouldn't go out until you ....

6 You mustn't make the tea until the water ....

7 You shouldn't get dressed until your mother ....

8 You shouldn't leave the table until everyone ....

6 **About you**

Complete this paragraph about your own future.

I'll live with my parents until I get married. ....

I'll look for a job as soon as ....

I'll get married when ....

I won't have any children until ....

I'll go to .... before ....

I'll .... after ....

16 may and might

FUN Magazine

We may have time machines

We recently asked a group of young people to give us their opinions about life in the future. This is what they said.

Raffaella
(12, Italy)

Anna
(10, Greece)

Hiroshi
(12, Japan)

If people stop fighting each other, then the future will be great. If there are still wars, then the future won't be good for a lot of people.

I'm looking forward to the future. I think I may become an astronaut. If I do, then I might be able to travel to Mars or to Venus.

I think the future is exciting. In the future we may have time machines. We might travel back to the past for our holidays!

What do YOU think about the future? Do you agree with Raffaella, Anna or Hiroshi? Write to *FUN Magazine* and give us your opinion.

Affirmative	Negative	
	Full form	**Short form**
I may / might go	I may / might not go	I mightn't go
you may / might go	you may / might not go	you mightn't go
he may / might go etc.	he may / might not go etc.	he mightn't go etc.

1 We use the modal verbs **may / might** (+ the bare infinitive) to express likelihood or possibility: **We *may / might go* to the USA next year.**

2 We can also use **may** to give permission: **He *may have* the book. / You *may not stay up* late.** (We *cannot* use **might** with this meaning.)

1 *Read the text again and correct these sentences.*

1 Anna may become a doctor. ...... *Wrong. She may become an astronaut.* ......

2 She may travel to Jupiter. ....

3 Hiroshi says people may have robots in the future. ....

4 He says we might travel to the future for our holidays. ....

5 Hiroshi doesn't think we will have time machines. ....

2 *Rewrite these sentences using* **may** *or* **might**.

Definite	Not as definite
1 He won't come.	He may not come. / He might not come.
2 We'll visit them next week.	....
3 She won't see him today.	....
4 I'll buy a new car.	....
5 My parents will buy me a	....
computer for my birthday.	....
6 I will not go to school	....
tomorrow.	....

Asking for and giving permission		
Interrogative	**Short answers**	
	Affirmative	**Negative**
May / Might / Can I go now?	Yes, you may.	No, you may not.
May / Might / Can we stay?	Yes, you can.	No, you can't.

may and **might** (or **can**) can both be used to ask for permission, but only **may** or **can** can be used in the short answer: **May / Might I ...? No, you may not / can't.**

3 *Write the questions with* **may** *or* **might** *and complete the short answers using* **may, can** *or* **can't**.

1 I / borrow / your book?

  May I borrow your book? .... — Of course you can. ....

2 we / come / with you?

  .... — Certainly ....

3 I / spend / the night here?

  .... — No, I'm sorry, ...

4 we / watch / TV / now?

  .... — Yes, ...

4 **About you**

Write a letter to FUN Magazine *and give your opinion about future schools, work, space travel and meeting people from other planets. Use* **may** *and* **might** *as often as you can. Write your letter on a separate piece of paper.*

17 Exclamations with *What ... !* and *How ... !*

What a great idea!

> The teachers of the school have decided
> t̶o̶ o̶r̶g̶a̶n̶i̶s̶e̶ a̶l̶l̶ i̶n̶t̶e̶r̶e̶s̶t̶e̶d̶ D̶i̶s̶c̶o̶ u̶a̶ l̶a̶t̶a̶

Guess what the notice says.

The teachers of the school have decided

a to give the children an extra week's holiday this year.

b to organise a disco for all the children this Saturday.

c that the children must do a lot of homework during the summer holidays this year.

Exclamations with nouns and with adjectives

What ... !	How ... !
What a good idea!	How terrible!
What an awful day!	How awful!
What awful shoes!	How fantastic!
What bad luck!	How stupid!
What terrible weather!	How wonderful!

In exclamations with **What** and **How**, we use:
What with a noun (or an adjective + a noun), and **How** with an adjective: **What a stupid idea! How stupid!**

---

1 *The children and their parents feel differently about the notice. Cover the picture above. Do these exclamations come from children or parents? Put them in the correct column.*

	Children	Parents
1 How terrible!	How terrible!	....
2 What a great idea!	....	....
3 How awful!	....	....
4 What bad luck!	....	....
5 What sensible teachers!	....	....
6 How wonderful!	....	....

2 *Say and write the exclamations. Write* **What** *or* **How.**

1 ...How......... beautiful!   4 .... a lovely day!

2 .... beautiful babies!   5 .... kind of you!

3 .... wonderful weather!   6 .... exciting!

3 *Do these exclamations need an article? Write it in if necessary.*

1 What ....*a*.... great film!   4 What .... awful man!

2 What .... nice girls!   5 What .... brilliant idea!

3 What .... lovely weather!   6 What .... good news!

4 *Complete two exclamations to fit each of the pictures.*

1 What *terrible weather*!

2 How *disappointing*......!

5 ....!

6 ....!

3 What ....!

4 How ....!

7 ....!

8 ....!

5 **About you**

What might you say in these situations with **What ... !** *or* **How ... ! ?**

1 A neighbour shows you her new baby.   What *a beautiful baby*......!

2 A friend suggests going to the cinema.   What ....!

3 A teacher gives you a lot of homework.   How ....!

4 A friend shows you her new jeans.   ....!

5 You are given an extra day off school.   ....!

6 Your aunt sends you some money.   ....!

They'd all been there before Columbus arrived

1 Most people think that Christopher Columbus discovered America in 1492. In fact, many other explorers had been there before him. The Chinese, Irish, Vikings and Welsh had all made journeys to America before Columbus arrived there.

2 In AD 459 a Chinese explorer had sailed across the Pacific to Mexico.

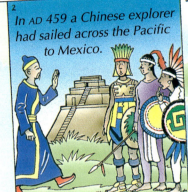

3 The Irish had made several journeys to the Atlantic coast in the sixth and seventh centuries.

ATLANTIC OCEAN

4 The Vikings had probably first reached America in the tenth century and possibly built a village there in the eleventh century.

5 In the twelfth century a Welsh prince had landed in America and had made contact with an Indian tribe. Until recently the people in that tribe still used boats that looked like traditional Welsh boats!

6 So people from many different lands had got to America before Columbus 'discovered' it.

Affirmative		Negative	
Full form	**Short form**	**Full form**	**Short form**
I had washed	I'd washed	I had not washed	I hadn't washed
you had washed	you'd washed	you had not washed	you hadn't washed
he had washed	he'd washed	he had not washed	he hadn't washed
etc.	etc.	etc.	etc.

1 We form the past perfect simple with **had** + past participle: **had done.**

2 We use it to describe an action which finished before another action in the past: **The plane *had already left* when we arrived at the airport.** (= The plane left. Then we arrived.)

3 NOTE: the past perfect of the verb **have** is **had had: I went home after I *had had* a meal in a restaurant.**

1 *Read the text again and complete these sentences, putting the verb in brackets into the past perfect simple.*

1 Many explorers .... *had got* .... to America before Columbus 'discovered' it.   (get)

2 A Chinese explorer .... to Mexico hundreds of years before Columbus discovered America.   (sail)

3 The Vikings .... a colony in America before anyone else did.   (probably build)

4 The Irish .... the Atlantic coast about 1,000 years before Columbus.   (already reach)

5 A Welsh prince .... contact with an Indian tribe three centuries before Columbus left Spain.   (already make)

Interrogative	Short answers	
	Affirmative	**Negative**
had I washed?	Yes, I had.	No, I hadn't.
had you washed?	Yes, you had.	No, you hadn't.
had he washed?	Yes, he had.	No, he hadn't.
etc.	etc.	etc.

Short answers to past perfect simple questions use **had / hadn't** (NOT ~~did / didn't~~): **Yes, I had. / No, I hadn't.**

2 *Make questions with the words given. Use the past perfect simple.*

1 she / already do / her homework / before they had dinner?
   Had she already done her homework before they had dinner?

2 the train / leave / when / you got to the station?
   ....

3 the rain / stop / when you left the house?
   ....

4 anyone / get to / China before Marco Polo?
   ....

5 the film / already start / when you got to the cinema?
   ....

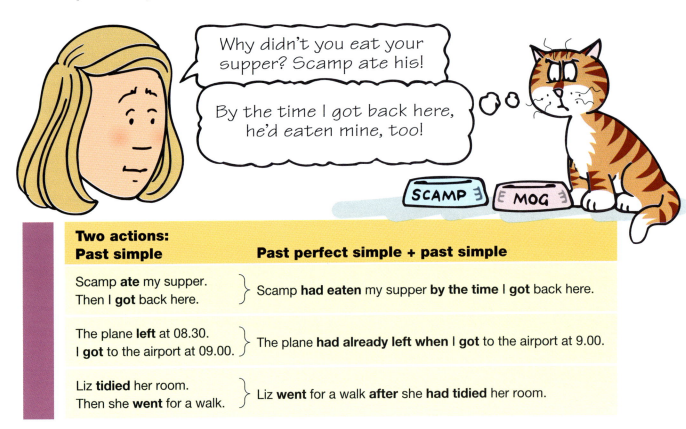

Two actions: Past simple	Past perfect simple + past simple
Scamp **ate** my supper. Then I **got** back here.	Scamp **had eaten** my supper **by the time** I **got** back here.
The plane **left** at 08.30. I **got** to the airport at 09.00.	The plane **had already left when** I **got** to the airport at 9.00.
Liz **tidied** her room. Then she **went** for a walk.	Liz **went** for a walk **after** she **had tidied** her room.

The sequence of past perfect simple and simple past tenses in a sentence tell us the order of actions in the past:

He cleaned his teeth *after* he had had a bath.

OR He had had a bath *before* he cleaned his teeth.

= 1 He had a bath ... and then 2 he cleaned his teeth.

3 *Join the sentences. Leave out* **then** *and use the word(s) in brackets.*

1 The train left. Then we arrived at the station.　(when)

The train had left when we arrived at the station.

2 She went to bed. Then her father came home from work.　(by the time)

....

3 He had dinner. Then he read his comic book.　(after)

....

4 They didn't drive far. Then their car broke down.　(when)

....

5 We did our homework. Then we went to the cinema.　(before)

....

6 They landed on the planet. Then they came out of the spaceship.　(as soon as)

....

4 *Complete the sentences with one of the following verbs or phrases. Put the verb into the correct tense, the past perfect simple or the past simple.*

> never taste ✔   be   already begin   never see   get

1 We _had never tasted_ Greek food before our holiday in Greece.

2 The film .... by the time we arrived at the cinema.

3 Her sister had already eaten all the ice-cream when she .... home.

4 They .... lions before they went to the zoo.

5 The teacher .... very angry because I hadn't done my homework.

5 *Choose the correct form, **a** or **b**, to complete the sentence.*

1 Columbus _discovered_ America in 1492.

   a discovered   **b** had discovered

2 The guests .... by the time we got there.

   a already left   **b** had already left

3 Paul and Mary .... five new books last week.

   a bought   **b** had bought

4 She .... washing the dishes by three o'clock.

   a finished   **b** had finished

6 *Mike made some notes for a composition about an experience he had some time ago. Write Mike's story using the past simple or the past perfect simple. Join the sentences using the words in parentheses.*

> first school trip (and) very excited.
>
> (As soon as) mother made favourite
>
> sandwiches — put them in rucksack.
>
> (After) packed everything — went to bed.
>
> (But) never went on trip
>
> (because when) get to school — bus
>
> already left.
>
> forgot to set alarm (when) went to bed.

It was my first school trip and I was very excited. As soon as my mother

....

....

....

....

....

....

19 Past perfect continuous

FUN Magazine

He'd been looking at the sights

We asked readers to tell us about their holiday experiences. This is what happened to Chris and Ben when they went to a town in Spain.

Chris had been to the town before but Ben hadn't. They were walking round the town when suddenly Chris noticed that Ben had disappeared. Chris couldn't understand it. They had been walking along the main street. Chris had been pointing out the sights to Ben. They'd been talking to each other but Chris had been talking more than Ben and he hadn't really been listening to him. Where had he gone? Chris returned to the hotel and waited for his friend.

Four hours later, Ben arrived at the hotel. What had he been doing for the last four hours? And why were there bandages on his head? Ben had been looking at the sights and listening to his friend. He hadn't noticed that some workmen had been digging a hole in the street. He had fallen into the hole. Chris had been talking to himself for about five minutes after Ben had fallen into the hole!

Affirmative	Negative
Full form / Short form	**Full form / Short form**
I had / I'd been playing	I had not / I hadn't been playing
you had / you'd been playing	you had not / you hadn't been playing
he had / he'd been playing	he had not / he hadn't been playing
etc.	etc.

We use the past perfect continuous to emphasise the duration of an action that was happening when another action occurred:
He *had been waiting* at the station *for half an hour* when the train came.
(= He started waiting half an hour ago and was still waiting when the train came.)

1 *Ask and answer these questions about the story.*
Write complete sentence answers.

1 Where had Chris and Ben been walking when Ben disappeared? *They had been*
   walking along the main street in a town in Spain.

2 What had Chris been pointing out to Ben? ....

   ....

3 What had they been doing as they looked at the sights? ....

   ....

4 Who had been talking more? ....

   ....

5 What had some workmen been doing? ....

   ....

6 Why hadn't Ben noticed the hole? ....

   ....

Interrogative	Short answers	
	Affirmative	**Negative**
had I been working?	Yes, I had.	No, I hadn't.
had you been working?	Yes, you had.	No, you hadn't.
had he been working?	Yes, he had.	No, he hadn't.
etc.	etc.	etc.

2 *Gran arrived at one o'clock yesterday.*
Look at the pictures , then ask and
answer questions. What had everyone
been doing? and for how long? Write
your questions and answers (like the
example) on a separate piece of paper.

1 Started 12 o'clock   2 Started 9 o'clock

3 Started 11 o'clock   4 Started 10 o'clock

1 *Had Dad been watching TV*
   before Gran arrived?
   No, he hadn't. He had been
   chopping vegetables for an
   hour when she arrived.

20 Direct and indirect statements

He says that he's thirsty

JANE: I can read animals' minds.

MIKE: You say you can read animals' minds? I don't believe you.

JANE: I can. Look at Scamp. I'm reading his mind now.

MIKE: OK. What's he thinking about?

I'm hungry.

He says that he's thirsty.

I've had a good breakfast.

He says he's had a good lunch.

I'd like to have a sleep now.

He says he'd like to go for a walk.

Jane's silly.

And he thinks I'm wonderful.

You're right, Mike. She can't read animals' minds!

Reporting simple tense statements with *say* and *tell*

Direct statements	Indirect statements
JANE: 'Scamp is hungry.'	→ Jane **says (that) Scamp is** hungry.
MIKE: 'I can't read animals' minds.'	→ Mike **says (that) he can't read** animals' minds.
LIZ AND JASON: 'We like climbing trees.'	→ They **tell me (that) they like** climbing trees.
MIKE: 'I didn't believe Jane.'	→ Mike **tells Jason (that) he didn't believe** Jane.
MUM: 'John's got a surprise for Dad.'	→ Mum **says (that) John's got** a surprise for Dad.

1 When we change direct statements into indirect statements we use the reporting verbs **say** and **tell** and (optionally) the word **that**.

2 The verb **say** does not usually take an indirect object: **He says (that) he is hungry.** But the verb **tell** always takes an indirect object: **He tells us [= to us] (that) he is hungry.**

3 When the reporting verb **say** or **tell** is in the present, any verb or verbs in the following part of the sentence stay the same as in the original direct speech.

---

1 *Answer these questions about the text.*

1 Does Jane say: 'I can read people's minds'?

No, she doesn't. She says that she can read animals' minds.

2 Does Mike tell Jane: 'I believe you'?

....

3 Does Jane say: 'Scamp's hungry'?

....

4 Does Scamp say: 'I've had a good lunch'?

....

5 Does Scamp think: 'Jane's wonderful'?

....

Reporting continuous tense statements with *say* and *tell*

Direct statements	Indirect statements
MIKE: 'We're going to town.'	➜ Mike **says (that) they are going** to town.
DAD: 'I was working all day.'	➜ Dad **says (that) he was working** all day.
JOHN: 'Tom has been learning French for three years.'	➜ John **tells me (that) Tom has been learning** French for three years.
JASON: 'Liz had been waiting for hours before John came.'	➜ Jason **says (that) Liz had been waiting** for hours before John came.

2 *Complete the indirect statements.*

1 'I'm going to Portugal soon.'

She says that she's going to Portugal soon...........

2 'I've been ironing for hours.'

Kate says ....

3 'I'll buy you the new Bon Jovi album.'

John tells Liz ....

4 'We were sitting in the garden when we saw him.'

They say ....

5 'I'll go to university if I pass my exams.'

She tells everyone ....

3 *When Jane comes home, she finds a note from John. On a separate piece of paper, finish writing what the note says. Start each sentence with 'It says that ...':*

The note says that Mum is
shopping in town. It says that

Jane,
Mum is shopping in town. Liz has been studying for hours and has gone for a walk. Scamp and Mog were playing in the garden when I left. They'd like their dinner now. We'll be back around 8.

John

Mike doesn't believe that you can read animals' minds, and I think he's right. Scamp is obviously asking you for a piece of your sandwich and you aren't giving him any.

I think / believe that ..., he knows that ..., she doesn't think that ...

'Scamp is hungry, I think.'	I **think (that)** Scamp **is** hungry. Jason **believes (that)** Scamp **is** hungry.
'They're coming.'	I **know (that) they're coming**. He **knows (that) they're coming**.
'He won't speak to me again.'	I **don't think (that) he will speak** to me again. She **doesn't believe (that) he will speak** to her again.

1 We use the verbs **think, know** and **believe** to introduce indirect statements just like **say** and **tell**.
2 Note how we usually make indirect negative statements with **think** and **believe**: I **don't think (that) he's English.** (NOT ~~I think that he isn't English.~~) / I **don't believe (that) you know him.** (NOT ~~I believe that you don't know him.~~)

4 *What do these people* know, believe *or* think?

1 'I'm very clever.'   He thinks *that he's very clever.*

2 'I don't study enough.'   Rita knows ....

3 'I can do better.'   He believes ....

4 'We won't win.'   They don't think ....

5 'He won't pass the test.'   I don't believe ....

6 'The goldfish is unhappy today.'   Jane thinks ....

7 'They don't work hard enough.'

   Miss Wall doesn't think ....

8 'John loves football.'   Everyone knows ....

5 Look at the pictures and write two indirect statements for each.
Start with the words in brackets.

1

I must lose weight.

(say) He says that he must lose weight.

(know) He knows that he must lose weight.

2

I want to be an astronaut.

(say) ....

....

(tell everybody) ....

....

3

This is the best book I've ever written.

(think) ....

....

(believe) ....

....

4

We didn't do very well in the test today.

(say) ....

....

(know) ....

....

6 You wrote your penfriend Peggy a short letter. She's reading your letter to her mother. What does she say? Write on a separate piece of paper and start each sentence with She says or He says.

Mum, I've just got a letter
from ... . He / She says (that)
he / she is coming ...

Dear Peggy,

Guess what! I'm coming to England in the summer. I've been saving all winter for these holidays. I've now got enough money. I kept it a secret because I wanted to surprise you. I'm looking forward to seeing you!

Love

She wants to know where you live

MRS CROFT: Where do you live, Jane?
JANE: What did your Mum say?
SARAH: She wants to know where you live.
JANE: Tell her I live in The Avenue.

MRS CROFT: Is this your road?
JANE: What did your Mum ask?
SARAH: She wants to know if this is your road.

MRS CROFT: Which house is yours?
JANE: What did your Mum say?
SARAH: She wants to know which house is yours.

MRS CROFT: Is it the white house?
JANE: What did she ask?
SARAH: She wants to know whether it's the white house.

I often wonder how the kids find their way home every day.

Direct questions	Indirect questions (reporting verbs in the present)
Is it the white house?	→ She wants to know **if / whether it is** the white house.
Do you like apples?	→ He'd like to know **if / whether you like** apples.
Can he skate well?	→ I wonder **if / whether he can skate** well.
Where are my shoes?	→ I'd like to know **where my shoes are**.
What should I do?	→ I wonder **what I should do**.
When can we swim?	→ Can you tell me **when we can swim**?

If you want to change a direct 'open question' into an indirect one with the introductory verb in the present, you must
1 use a verb like **ask, wonder, want to know,** etc.
2 put in **if** or **whether** after the introductory verb
3 make necessary changes to pronouns, possessive adjectives, etc.
4 put the verb of the indirect question in the affirmative and in the same tense.
   It is not in the question form. John: **Are they at home?'** → John wants to know **if/whether they are at home.**

1 *Look at the text again and complete these sentences.*

1 Firstly, Mrs Croft wants to know *where Jane lives.* ....

2 Then Mrs Croft wants to know ....

3 Then Mrs Croft wants to know ....

4 Finally, ...

2 *Gran is asking Mike some questions. Change her questions from direct to indirect questions.*

1 How old are you?

I'd like to know how old you are.

2 When is your teacher's birthday?

I wonder ....

3 Can you play football well?

I want to know ....

4 What are your sisters interested in?

Can you tell me ....

5 Will your exam results be good this year?

I wonder ....

Direct questions	Indirect questions
Did you meet Sue?	➜ He wants to know **if / whether you met** Sue.
Have you been there?	➜ She'd like to know **if / whether you have been** there.
Is he going to be there?	➜ I wonder **if / whether he is going to be** there.
Can you help me?	➜ I'd like to know **if / whether you can help** me.
Was she at home?	➜ Can you tell me **if / whether she was at home**?

3 *Change some more of Gran's questions to indirect questions.*

1 Was your mother born in London?

I wonder if your mother was born in London.

2 Did you do well at school last year?

I'd like to know ....

3 Have your parents ever been to the USA?

I wonder ....

4 Can you play chess with me tonight?

I'd like to know ....

5 Have you played tennis this week?

I want to know ....

Direct questions	Indirect questions
Where did Jane go yesterday? ➜	**She wonders where Jane went** yesterday.
Why does he often sit here? ➜	**I wonder why he often sits** here.
What have they done? ➜	**I'd like to know what they have done.**
How do I get there? ➜	**Can you tell me how I get** there?
How often had they met? ➜	**Do you know how often they had met**?

If you want to change a direct 'closed question' into an indirect one with the introductory verb in the present, you must do the same as on page 57, but instead of **if / whether**, you use the question word of the question you are reporting: John: '**Where are they?**' ➜ John wants to know **where they are.**

4 *Direct questions can sometimes sound rude to English people. Make these questions more polite in two different ways.*

1 When does the train leave?

..*Can you tell me when the train leaves?*..............................

..*Do you know when the train leaves?*...............................

2 Which restaurant would you recommend?

Can ....

Do ....

3 What can we do in the evenings in this town?

Can ....

Do ....

4 What should we see in this town?

Can ....

Do ....

5 How much does a single room cost?

Can ....

Do ....

5 *What is the man asking in each of these pictures?*

1

Excuse me. Can you tell me where the station is?

2

Excuse me. Do ....

3

Excuse me. Can ....

6 *Each of these sentences has one mistake. Write the sentences correctly.*

1 I want to know when does the flight from Amsterdam arrive.

I want to know when the flight from Amsterdam arrives.

2 Can you tell me where Jane did go yesterday?

....

3 Jane would like to know did you stay at home yesterday.

....

4 I wonder whether is there a post office near here.

....

5 I wonder how much did you pay for that enormous ice-cream.

....

7 *Fill in the gaps to complete the crossword.*

1 I .... to know where she lives.

2 Do you know .... old she is?

3 Can you .... me what the time is?

4 She says .... she is good at chess.

5 I wonder .... he left so early.

6 Do you know .... the train will leave?

7 Jane .... when they'll meet again.

8 I'd like to know .... he passed his test.

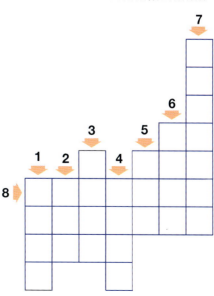

Reported speech after *said*, *told*, *asked*, *wanted to know*

She also said I was handsome!

Do you like going to the cinema?

It depends on the film.

What kind of films do you like?

Comedies and cowboy films.

LIZ: Did you enjoy the disco last night?
JOHN: Yeah, it was great! A girl asked me if I liked going to the cinema.
LIZ: What did you say?
JOHN: I told her that it depended on the film. Then she asked me what kind of films I liked.
LIZ: What did you tell her?
JOHN: I said that I liked comedies and cowboy films. She also said I was handsome!

Direct statements	Reported statements (reporting verbs in the past)
'Jo *is* a clever girl.'	➜ John *said* (that) Jo *was* a clever girl.
'We *live* in London.'	➜ They *told us* (that) they *lived* in London.
'I *met* Jane in the park.'	➜ Jason *said* (that) he *had met* Jane in the park.
'I *have finished* my work.'	➜ Dad *told them* (that) he *had finished* his work.
'I'*ll come* on Sunday.'	➜ He *said* (that) he *would come* on Sunday.
'I *can swim*.'	➜ She *told us* (that) she *could swim*.

1 When we report statements in the past after **said / told,** we use the optional word **that**.
2 We make certain changes to personal pronouns etc: **'I am a clever cat,' said Mog.** **➜ Mog said (that) he was a clever cat.**
3 Tenses of verbs change. They move one tense back from the original sentence: **is ➜ was, lives ➜ lived, has finished ➜ had finished,** etc.
4 The tenses after the verbs **think, know, believe,** etc. also change when they are in the past: **He thought (that) you lived in London.**

1 *Complete these statements about the text with* **said** *or* **told.**

1 John .....*told*..... Liz that he had met a girl at the disco.

2 John .... that he had enjoyed himself at the disco.

3 John .... the girl that he liked comedies.

4 He .... that he liked cowboy films, too.

5 The girl .... that John was handsome.

6 John .... her he liked comedies and cowboy films.

7 She .... him that he was handsome.

2 *Fill in the missing words to complete the reported statements.*

1 Teacher to Mum: 'Liz is very good at French.'

The teacher told Mum <u>that Liz was very good</u> at French.

2 Helen: 'I've known them for years.'

Helen said .... them for years.

3 My friends to me: 'You can stay with us.'

My friends told me .... with them.

4 The children: 'We'll save money for our trip to Europe.'

The children said .... money for their trip to Europe.

5 Girl to her mother: 'John was very polite.'

The girl told her mother .... very polite.

6 Mike to me: 'I don't like tennis much.'

Mike told me .... tennis much.

7 Mary: 'He wrote me a long letter.'

Mary said .... a long letter.

8 They: 'We haven't seen the film.'

They said .... the film.

9 Jane to me: 'I'll be at school early tomorrow.'

Jane .... early tomorrow.

10 Jason to us: 'Jane can paint very well.'

Jason .... very well.

MUM: What did the dentist ask you, Jane?

JANE: He asked me if I brushed my teeth regularly. He wanted to know what toothpaste I used. And then he asked if I ate many sweets.

MUM: Did you tell him the truth, Jane?

JANE: I didn't tell him anything. I couldn't speak with my mouth open!

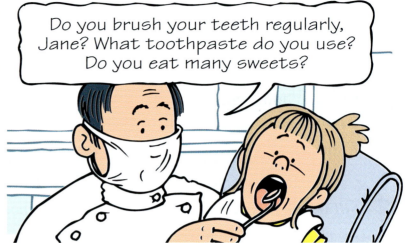

Do you brush your teeth regularly, Jane? What toothpaste do you use? Do you eat many sweets?

Direct questions	Reported questions (with reporting verbs in the past)
'Are you happy?' he asked us.	➜ He asked us if we were happy.
'Have you seen that film yet?' she asked me.	➜ She asked me whether I had seen that film yet.
'Can you swim?' I wanted to know.	➜ I wanted to know if they could swim.
'How are you?' he asked me.	➜ He asked me how I was.
'Where have you been?' Mum asked.	➜ Mum asked Liz where she had been.
'What toothpaste do you use?' the dentist asked me.	➜ The dentist asked me what toothpaste I used.

When we report questions with the reporting verb in the past (**asked, wanted to know**),

1 we put **if** or **whether** after the introductory verb and before reported open questions;

2 we change the tense, the pronouns and posessive adjectives, etc;

3 we put the verb in the reported question in the affirmative form: **She wanted to know if he was ill**. (NOT '... if was he ill?')

4 When there is a question word in the direct question, we use that word instead of **if / whether**, and the verb is once again in the affirmative.

3 *There are mistakes in all these sentences.*
Underline the mistakes and write the correct forms.

1 We asked them <u>where were they from</u>.   *where they were from*

2 The teacher asked why hadn't I read the book.   ....

3 The new student asked who is our teacher.   ....

4 She asked me whether had I seen him.   ....

5 I asked him what time is it.   ....

6 We wanted to know where did they live.   ....

4 *Nick has taken an examination in English. What did Nick*
tell his friends? Report the questions the examiner asked him.

1 Do you like English?   She asked me *if I liked English.* ....

2 Do you find it difficult?   She wanted to know ....

3 Have you ever been to England?   and ....

4 What are your hobbies?   and ....

5 Can you describe the picture   And finally she ....
  on the wall?

5 *This report appeared in your school paper. Read it carefully, then*
write the actual words that the interviewer and George said.

George lived with his family in Germany for several years. They came back to Greece two months ago. (1) When I asked George whether he found life in Greece better than life in Germany, (2) he said he didn't really know because he hadn't been in Greece long. (3) When I asked him if he missed Germany, (4) he told me he missed his friends and hoped he could visit them in the summer. (5) I wanted to know what sports he liked. (6) He said he swam and played football, but his favourite sport had

always been basketball. (7) I asked what his future plans were. (8) He said he wanted to become a professional basketball player.

INTERVIEWER: 1 Do you find life in Greece better than life in Germany?

GEORGE: 2 I don't really know *because I haven't been here long.*

INTERVIEWER: 3 ....

GEORGE: 4 ....

INTERVIEWER: 5 ....

GEORGE: 6 ....

INTERVIEWER: 7 ....

GEORGE: 8 ....

23 so and such

Such a terrible day!

Dear Gran,

How are you? I hope you're well. I had such a terrible day yesterday that I thought I must write and tell you about it.

First of all I woke up so late that I didn't have time for breakfast. Then it was such a wet day here yesterday that everyone was wearing raincoats and carrying umbrellas. But I was so late that I didn't have time to look for my raincoat or my umbrella. When I got to school, I was so wet and hungry that I felt quite ill.

Then the teacher said she had a surprise for us! She said we had done our last mathematics test so badly that she wanted to give us another one. So, yesterday afternoon we had a mathematics test. It was so difficult that I could only answer half the questions.

We're all looking forward to seeing you soon.

Love,
Jane

so + adjective or adverb	**such + adjective + noun**
It's **so hot!** The girls are **so beautiful!** Don't walk **so fast!** It's **so cheap that** I'd like to buy two. We did our test **so badly that** our teacher gave us another one.	It's **such a hot day** today! They're **such beautiful girls!** It's **such hot weather!** It was **such a good film that** I went to see it three times. It was **such cheap ice-cream that** we had two each.

1 We use **so** with an adjective or adverb: **It was so good ... / He ran so fast ...**
2 We use **such** with an adjective and a noun: **such a hot day / such an awful day.** (Note that we use the indefinite article **a / an** with a singular noun.)
3 Note the construction **It was such a hot day that we all wore shorts. / He walked so slowly that he missed his bus.**

1 *Correct these statements about the text.*

1 Jane had such a good day yesterday that she wrote and told Gran about it.
   Wrong. Jane had such a terrible day yesterday that she wrote and told Gran about it.

2 Jane woke up so early that she had lots of time for breakfast.
   ....

3 It was such a hot day that everyone was wearing shorts.
   ....

4 Jane was so cold that she felt quite ill.

....

5 The test was so easy that Jane could answer all the questions.

....

2 *Write* **so** *or* **such** *before these exclamations. Add* **a** *or an* **if necessary.**

1 It's .....*so*..... hot here!

2 It's .*such a*. hot day today!

3 Liz can be .... funny girl!

4 He is .... rude!

5 It was .... awful weather last week!

6 The children were all wearing .... dirty jeans!

7 You are .... clever!

3 *Change these from* **so** *sentences to* **such** *sentences, or* **such** *to* **so.** *Make all the necessary changes.*

1 Mike is so nice that everyone likes him.

Mike is such a nice boy that everyone likes him..............................

2 It is such a wet day today that we can't go to the beach.

....

3 Liz is so naughty that her mother often gets annoyed with her.

....

4 This is such a difficult exercise that I'd like you to help me.

....

5 The day was so lovely that we took a picnic to the park.

....

4 **About you**

Add **so** *or* **such** *and complete this paragraph about one of your friends in any appropriate way.*

My friend is ....*so*..... good at ....*art*.... that *she won a prize last year*...............

but she / he is .... bad at .... that ....

....

My friend is .... a nice person that ....

She / He .... well that ....

....

FUN Magazine

What would you do if you were rich?

Most people would like to be rich. They think: 'If I were rich, I wouldn't have any problems. I'd be able to buy everything I wanted and I wouldn't worry about the future.' But there would be one problem: How would you spend your money?

If someone gave you a small amount of money, would you
- a) buy a computer? ☐
- b) buy lots of new clothes? ☐
- c) organise a party? ☐
- d) do something else? (say what) ....

If you won quite a lot of money, would you
- a) go to Disneyland in France or the USA? ☐
- b) buy yourself and your friends new bikes? ☐
- c) save it? ☐
- d) do something else? (say what) ....

If you were very rich, would you
- a) give your money to poor people? ☐
- b) buy a jet plane? ☐
- c) buy a Greek island? ☐
- d) do something else? (say what) ....

Type 2 Conditional sentences

If **I won** a lot of money,	I **would travel** / I'**d travel** round the world.
She **would buy** / she'**d buy** lots of new clothes	if she **won** a lot of money.
If you **didn't eat** so many sweets,	you **wouldn't be** sick.
He **wouldn't be** happy	if he **had** a lot of money.
If they **had** enough money,	they **could go** on the school trip.
If **I was / were** rich,	I **would help** / I'**d help** poor people.
If Dad **wasn't / weren't** here,	I **wouldn't do** my homework!

1 We use 2nd Conditional sentences to describe a situation (general present or future) which is unlikely to occur immediately or which is clearly a fantasy:
If I *had* a million pounds, I *would be* very happy!

2 Look at the ideas   He doesn't write things down so he forgets them.
and the form: ***If he wrote* things down, *he wouldn't forget* them.**

3 A Conditional sentence can begin with the main clause or the **if**-clause: if it begins with the **if**-clause, it must have a comma before the main clause.

4 Modal verbs in the **if**-half of a 2nd Conditional sentence will be in the past:
can ➜ could, must ➜ had to, etc.

5 When the verb **be** appears in the **if**-half of a 2nd Conditional, we can use **was / were** in the 1st / 3rd person: ***If I was / were* you, I'd stay here.**

1 *When you have done the* FUN Magazine *quiz, ask and answer these questions. Then write your true answers in complete sentences.*

1 What would you do if someone gave you a small amount of money?

If someone gave me a small amount of money, I'd buy a computer.

Now you: If someone ....

....

2 What would you do if you won quite a lot of money?

If I ....

....

3 What would you do if you were very rich?

....

....

2 *Say and write these sentences again using Conditional 2. Make any other necessary changes.*

1 Dad is very busy today so he won't play golf.

If Dad *weren't so busy today, he would play golf.* ....

2 He isn't tall so he can't be a basketball player.

If he ....

3 My house doesn't have a garden so I don't grow my own vegetables.

If my house ....

4 I can't work on a computer so I won't get the job.

If I ....

5 The weather is bad so we'll stay at home.

If the weather ....

6 I don't live in a big flat so I don't have a dog.

If I ....

7 We haven't got any bread so we won't make any sandwiches.

If we ....

8 Dad doesn't like cold weather so he won't visit Iceland.

If Dad ....

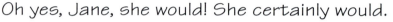

What would your life be like if you were a famous artist? Would you be happy?

Of course, I would. I'd travel round the world, I'd give interviews, I would do all sorts of things, and Mum wouldn't be angry with her famous daughter if she didn't behave.

Oh yes, Jane, she would! She certainly would.

Interrogative	Short answers	
	Affirmative	**Negative**
Would you live in the country if you could?	Yes, I would.	No, I wouldn't.
Would he help me if he were here?	Yes, he would.	No, he wouldn't.
Would she come if I asked her?	Yes, she would.	No, she wouldn't.
If we were late, would they be angry?	Yes, they would.	No, they wouldn't.
What would you do if you had $1,000,000?	I'd buy an aeroplane.	
If you could be somebody else, who would you like to be?	I'd like to be the best footballer in the world.	

3 *Put the verbs in the right form to complete the questions. Then answer the questions.*

1 If you could be someone else, who / you like / to be?

    If you could be someone else, who would you like to be?

    I'd like to be Einstein.

2 If you came to class late, what / your teacher / say?

    ....

    ....

3 If you took a trip around Europe, how / you / travel?

    ....

    ....

4 If you could live somewhere else, where / you / live?

    ....

    ....

5 If you chose a car for your father, what car / you / choose?

    ....

    ....

4 *Look at the pictures and say what you* **would do in these situations.**

1

If you were ill?

If I were ill, I would go to the doctor.

2

If you could fly in a spaceship?

....

....

3

If you were a famous writer?

....

....

4

If you saw a ghost?

....

....

5
If you met Tom Cruise?

....

....

6
If you had a time machine?

....

....

5 *Choose the correct verbs to complete the paragraph.*

could save   wouldn't be ✔   didn't buy   used   picked up
wouldn't cut down   collected ✔   wouldn't make

Our beaches are dirty because we leave empty cans and bottles on them. Our beaches (1) wouldn't be dirty if we (2) collected our own empty cans and bottles. To produce the paper for a single newspaper, we must cut down a few trees. If we (3) .... recycled paper, we (4) .... so many trees. Many sea animals think that plastic is food. They eat it and die. We (5) .... an animal's life if we (6) .... a plastic bag from the beach. Spray cans destroy our atmosphere. If we (7) .... spray cans, factories (8) .... them.

Lisa Young asks...

'What would YOU have done?'

1 Helen found a ten-pound note at a railway station.

What would you have done if you had found that ten-pound note? Would you have taken it to the lost property office? Or would you have kept it?

If she had found ten pence, she wouldn't have taken it to the lost property office. She would probably have kept it. But she found ten pounds, so she took it to the lost property office.

2 Helen invited Mary to stay at her house while her parents were away. The girls broke a very valuable vase.

What would you have done? Would you have kept quiet? Would you have told her parents at once? Would you have tried to mend the vase?

They didn't tell Helen's parents. They hid the pieces and hoped that her parents wouldn't notice for a long time. If the vase hadn't been so valuable, they would probably have told her parents.

Type 3 Conditional sentences

If she **had found** / she**'d found** ten pence,
    she **would have kept** / she**'d have kept** it.
I **would have taken** / I**'d have taken** it to the lost property office
    if I **had found** / I**'d found** it.
If they **had not broken** / they **hadn't broken** such an expensive vase,
    they **would have told** / they**'d have told** her parents.
They **would not have broken** / They **wouldn't have broken** the vase
    if they **had been** / they**'d been** more careful,

We use 3rd Conditional sentences to talk about situations which might have happened in the past, but didn't:

If she had found ten pence, she would have kept it.

(= She didn't find ten pence, so she didn't keep it.)

1 *Read the text again. Fill in the gaps in these sentences with the verbs in brackets in the correct form.*

1 If Helen (find) ......*had found*...... ten pence, she (keep) ...*would have kept*... it.

2 If Helen (find) .... twenty pounds, she (take) .... it to the lost property office.

3 If the vase (not be) .... so valuable, the girls (tell) .... Helen's parents the truth.

4 Helen and Mary (not hide) .... the vase if they (not break) .... it.

2 *Here are three more situations. What would YOU have done?*

1 John saw a little girl fall into a river. He jumped in to help her. Would you have jumped in? Would you have called 'Help'?

If *I had seen the girl, I wouldn't have jumped in because I can't swim, but I would have called 'Help!' very loudly.*

2 Sarah saw a little boy take some sweets from a shop without paying. She didn't say anything. What would you have done?

If ....
....

3 Pat won some money last year. She gave some to her sister and put the rest in the bank. Would you have done the same?

If ....
....

3 *Write these sentences out in full, using* **would** *or* **had** *instead of 'd.*

1 I'd have stayed at home if I'd known you were coming.
I would have stayed at home if I had known you were coming.

2 If Homer'd lived in the twentieth century, he'd have written for TV.
....

3 If she'd kept the money, she'd have felt awful.
....

4 I'd have helped you if you'd asked me.
....

JANE: Liz has eaten all the ice-cream. I wouldn't have done that, would I, Mum?

LIZ: Yes, you would. You didn't know Mum had bought some ice-cream. If you'd known, you'd have eaten it.

MUM: Did you eat all the sausages too, Liz?

LIZ: No, I didn't! It was Scamp.

JANE: Liz left the fridge door open. Would you have taken the sausages if she hadn't left the door open, Scamp?

No, I wouldn't. Thanks, Liz.

Interrogative	Short answers	
	Affirmative	**Negative**
Would you have kept the money if you had found it?	Yes, I would.	No, I wouldn't.
Would she have helped us if she had had the time?	Yes, she would.	No, she wouldn't.
If Liz hadn't left the door open, would Scamp have eaten the sausages?	Yes, he would.	No, he wouldn't.
If we had known him better, would we have invited him?	Yes, we would.	No, we wouldn't.

4 *Ask and answer questions using the words below and the third conditional tense. Then write the questions and short answers.*

1 Fritz found an old watch on the bus. He gave it to the driver.

If / he / find / a **gold** watch / on the bus, / he / keep / it?

If he had found a gold watch on the bus, would he have kept it?

Yes, he would.

2 Helen and Mary broke an expensive vase.

If / they / break / a **cheap** vase / they / tell / Helen's parents?

....

Yes, ...

3 You were born in the twentieth century and you ride a bike.

If / you / born / in the **sixteenth** century, / you / ride / a bike?

....

No, ...

5 *Look at these sentences.*

> **Liz didn't go** to town with the others, **so she didn't enjoy herself**.
>
> But **IF she had gone** to town with the others, **she would have enjoyed herself**.

Now rewrite these sentences in the same way.

1 John did well in his exams, so Dad was happy.

   If John hadn't done well in his exams, Dad wouldn't have been happy.

2 Liz left the fridge door open, so Scamp took the sausages.

   If Liz ....

3 Scamp ate too many sausages, so he was sick.

   If Scamp ....

4 Jane woke up late, so she missed the bus for school.

   If Jane ....

6 *Are these questions second or third conditional questions? Put the verb in brackets in the correct form — would do, would have done, did or had done.*

1 What (you do) would you do if you (win) won a lot of money?

2 What (you do) .... if you (meet) .... your

   teacher at the cinema last Friday?

3 What (Liz eat) .... yesterday if Mum (not buy) ....

   some ice-cream?

4 If Mog (catch) .... a mouse next week, ...

   (Mum be) angry?

7 **About you**

Complete this paragraph. How would your life have been different if you had been born in England? Use the verbs at the side of the page.

If I'd been born in England, English would have been .... | be

my first language. I .... the English | understand

language without any problems. I .... | go

to an English school. I .... English TV. | watch

But I .... my own language! | not speak

They picked out the same words

Do you know any twins? Twins are very interesting, especially if they have been <u>brought up</u> in different families. And some interesting experiments have been <u>carried out</u>.

Some time ago a psychologist <u>did</u> some experiments with two twins, Jane and Mary, who had been <u>raised</u> separately. He put them in different rooms. He then asked them to <u>pick out</u> three words from a list of 500 words and to look them up in a dictionary. Jane and Mary <u>chose</u> the same three words.

He then gave them the same five mathematics problems to <u>solve</u>. They <u>worked</u> them <u>out</u> at exactly the same time. They also made exactly the same mistake in one of the problems.

The psychologist couldn't understand it. When he reported the results of the experiments, other psychologists said that he <u>was making up</u> stories. They were sure he <u>was inventing</u> the experiments and the results.

In the end, the psychologist needed six months of psychological treatment himself!

Phrasal verbs with an object

Verb + particle + object (noun) or Verb + object (noun / pronoun) + particle

bring up (= raise)	**make up** (= invent)	**look up** (= find)
bring up the children	**make up** a story	**look up** a word
bring the children **up**	**make** a story **up**	**look** a word **up**
bring them **up**	**make** it **up**	**look** it **up**

call off (= cancel)	The game was **called off** because of the rain.
carry out (= do)	He **carried out** the experiments in the laboratory.
give away (= get rid of)	She had a lot of old books. She **gave** them **away**.
hold up (= delay)	She was **held up** in traffic. She came in late.
knock out (= make unconscious)	The woman hit the thief with her bag and **knocked** him **out**.
pick out (= choose)	The girls had to **pick** three words **out**.
put up (= give a bed to)	Can you **put** me **up** for the night?
work out (= solve)	They **worked out** the solutions to the problems.

1 *Look at the text. Five phrasal verbs are underlined. Five words with the same meaning as the phrasal verbs are also underlined. Write down the phrasal verbs and match them with their meanings.*

Phrasal verbs	Meanings
brought up	raised

2   *Add* away, out, off *or* up *to the sentences.*

1   Mum picked ..out........ a yellow dress to wear at the party.

2   The accident held the traffic .... on the motorway.

3   They called the wedding .... because the girl fell in love with another man.

4   Elvis Presley was brought .... in a very poor family.

5   Hans Christian Andersen made .... some of the world's best stories.

6   The boy picked .... the biggest apple and ate it.

7   A flower pot fell on the man's head and knocked him ....

8   I'm giving all my posters .... because I don't want them any more.

9   Where were you brought .... ?

10   Tomorrow's football match has been called .... The football pitch is too wet.

3   *Use the words in brackets to complete these sentences.*

1   Mum gave Jane a difficult puzzle but she worked it out

    very quickly.   (work out / it)

2   The team captain gave the instructions and the players

    ....   (carry out / them)

3   She couldn't find a hotel room so her friend

    ....   (put up / her)

4   We didn't know where Mount Fuji was so we

    .... in the encyclopedia.   (look up / it)

5   Mum found some skirts that she didn't want, so she

    ....   (give away / them)

6   Most of our friends can't come to the party, so let's

    ....   (call off / it)

7   There was a major accident on the road and it .... for an hour. (hold up / us)

8   The tall man stood up quickly and .... on the low ceiling! (knock out / himself)

Some phrasal verbs without an object

break down	Our car **broke down** on the motorway.
get up	He **got up** at six o'clock.
look out	**Look out**! There's a car coming!
ring off	She was smiling when she **rang off**.
set out	We don't want to be late, so we'll **set out** early.
stay up	The children usually **stay up** late on Saturdays.
take off	The plane **took off** a few minutes ago.
turn up	They had arranged to meet but Pat didn't **turn up**.

Certain phrasal verbs, like all of those in the box above, do not take an object. These verbs cannot be used in the passive.

4 *Match six of the sentences in the table above with these pictures.*

1

He got up at six o'clock.

2

....

....

3

....

....

4

....

....

5

....

....

6

....

....

5 *Put the words in brackets into the correct order to complete the sentences.*

1 The party began at eight, but *most of the guests turned up much later.*

   (much later / most of the guests / but / turned / up)

2 I didn't know what the word meant, so I ....

   (in the dictionary / it / looked / up)

3 We've been on the phone for over an hour so ....

   (must / I / ring / now / off)

4 It's a long journey, ...

   (we / early tomorrow morning / must set / so / out)

5 After looking through several books, ...

   (he / out / a detective story / picked)

6 I wouldn't believe her stories if I were you because ....

   (makes / them / she / up / often)

7 The pianist missed the plane, ...

   (was / off / so / the concert / called)

8 I'm coming to visit your town, so ....?

   (you / me / put / can / for a few days / up)

6 *Crossword Puzzle. The answers to the clues are phrasal verbs. The coloured part is for the particle of the phrasal verb.*

Across

   2 choose (4,3)
   4 arrive (4,2)
   6 stop working (e.g. car) (5,4)
   8 be awake later than usual (4,2)
  12 start a journey (3,3)
  13 leave the ground (4,3)

Down

   1 end a telephone conversation (4,3)
   3 do what you are asked
      to do (5,3)
   5 find a solution to a problem (4,3)
   7 cancel (4,3)
   9 give a bed for the night (3,2)
  10 invent (e.g. a story) (4,2)
  11 delay (4,2)

27 too, not ... either; So / Neither (do) I

I don't like Mr Evans either

LIZ: Who's your favourite teacher?

MIKE: Mrs Brown, I think. I like Mr Evans too.

LIZ: I don't like Mrs Brown. And I don't like Mr Evans either. I like Miss Wall.

MIKE: So do I. Miss Wall's nice. She gives us interesting lessons. I don't like Mr Briggs.

LIZ: Neither do I. His lessons are boring.

MIKE: I'd hate to be a teacher when I grow up.

LIZ: So would I.

Schoolchildren are terrible, aren't they?

Statement	Agreement too / not ... either	So ... / Neither ...
Affirmative		
I like pop music.	I like it **too**.	**So do I!**
I am fifteen.	I'm fifteen **too**.	**So am I!**
I went to Paris last year.	I went there **too**.	**So did I!**
Jack can swim.	Betty can swim **too**.	**So can Betty!**
You're looking well.	You're looking well **too**.	**So are you!**
Negative		
I don't speak Spanish.	I do**n't** speak it **either**.	**Neither do I!**
They aren't cold.	I'm **not** cold **either**.	**Neither am I!**
I didn't enjoy school.	I did**n't** enjoy it **either**.	**Neither did I!**
I would never do that.	I would**n't** do that **either**.	**Neither would I!**
They haven't got a car.	We have**n't** got one **either**.	**Neither have we!**

1 We use **too** and **So** to agree with affirmative ideas, **not ... either** and **Neither** to agree with negative ideas.

2 When we use **too** or **not ... either**, we repeat the sentence we are agreeing with and add the words: **I like it too. / I don't like it either.**

3 When we agree using **so** or **neither**, we start with that word and invert the subject and modal or helping verb: **So can I. / Neither do I.**

1 *Agree with these statements in two different ways.*

1 I love football.   <u>I love it too.</u>   <u>So do I.</u>

2 Liz likes some of her teachers.   ....

3 Mike's keen on stamps.   ....

4 I went to Jane's party.   ....

5 They can ski. ....

6 I'd like an apple. ....

7 Jane's got a mountain bike. ....

8 I'll be at home tomorrow. ....

2 *Agree with these statements in two different ways.*
Use the person or people in brackets.

1 Jane hasn't been to Moscow. (Liz)

Liz hasn't been to Moscow either. / Neither has Liz.

2 Liz and Mike don't want to be teachers. (Jane)

....

3 Mike isn't going to the cinema tonight. (Jason and Liz)

....

4 John can't play volleyball very well. (Mike)

....

5 Mum didn't eat any ice-cream. (Dad)

....

3 *John says these things. Do you agree or disagree?*
Write your agreement or disagreement.

1 I like cabbage. So do I! ... or I hate it!

2 I'm playing football this weekend. ....

3 I don't like going to the dentist. ....

4 I've been to Italy. ....

5 I can't play chess very well. ....

4 About you

Compare yourself and a friend. How do you feel about these
things — TV, homework, holidays, history, swimming, volleyball?
Use So *and* Neither, too *and* not ... either *sentences. Write on a*
separate piece of paper.

My friend, Eleni, likes cartoons on TV. So do I! She doesn't like news

programmes. I don't like them either.

28 both, all, neither, none, both ... and, neither ... nor, all of, some of, none of

FUN Magazine

Lisa Young finds out...

Both boys and girls enjoy sport!

I have been finding out how teenage boys and girls spend their time. I sent a questionnaire to 100 boys and 100 girls aged thirteen to sixteen. This is what I discovered:

- All teenagers — both boys and girls — prefer weekends to school-days. But girls like school-days more than boys do.

- Neither boys nor girls really like doing homework but girls spend more time doing homework than boys do.

- Almost all teenage girls spend at least an hour a week on the telephone.

- None of the teenagers who filled in the questionnaire like reading newspapers.

- But all of them enjoy filling in questionnaires.

- And all the girls who filled in this questionnaire said they enjoyed buying new clothes.

---

all, all (of) the, all of, some of, none, none of, both ... and, neither ... nor

All children need love.
All (of) the children here like watching television.
All (of) the men here play golf.
How many questions could you answer? — **None**!
Is there more coffee? — No, there is **none** left.
Both boys **and** girls like weekends.
Both Peter **and** Brian play tennis.

All of them like going to the cinema.
They all have the same teacher.
Some of them like their teacher a lot.
None of the men here play tennis.
None of them enjoy dancing.
Neither boys **nor** girls like school-days.
Neither Peter **nor** Brian plays golf.

---

1 *Read the text again and complete these sentences.*
Use all, all of, all (of) the, none of the, both ... and, neither ... nor.

1 ......All..... teenagers prefer weekends to school-days.

2 .... boys .... girls prefer weekends to school-days.

3 .... boys .... girls really like doing homework.

4 .... teenagers who filled in Lisa Young's questionnaire like reading newspapers.

5 .... them enjoy filling in questionnaires.

2 *Read the text again and correct these statements.*

1 Lisa's been finding out how just boys spend their time, hasn't she?
   No, she's been finding out how both boys and girls spend their time.

2 Only some teenagers prefer weekends, don't they?

....

3 None of the girls said they enjoyed buying new clothes.

....

3 *Here are some more questions from the questionnaire. Summarise the answers of the 200 students. Use* all (of) the, *or* none (of the).

Questions	Boys		Girls	
	Yes	No	Yes	No
1 Do you prefer comic books to teen magazines?	0	100	0	100
2 Do you prefer basketball to tennis?	100	0	100	0
3 Do you like fashion magazines?	0	100	100	0
4 Do you read sports magazines?	100	0	0	100

1 None of the students prefer comic books to teen magazines.

2 ....

3 ....

4 ....

4 *Join the sentences using* Both … and *or* Neither … nor.

1 Mum likes reading newspapers. Dad likes reading newspapers, too.
   Both Mum and Dad like reading newspapers.

2 Mike hasn't been to Oxford. Jason hasn't been to Oxford, either.
   Neither Mike nor Jason has been to Oxford.

3 Women enjoy dancing. Men enjoy dancing, too.

....

4 Dad didn't play golf yesterday. Peter didn't play golf yesterday, either.

....

5 Liz will ride her bike. Jane will ride her bike, too.

....

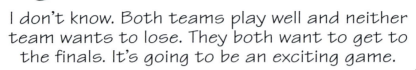

Good! Tonight England's playing Germany and Russia's playing Italy in the European Cup semi-finals. All four teams are very good.

Will England beat Germany, Dad?

I don't know. Both teams play well and neither team wants to lose. They both want to get to the finals. It's going to be an exciting game.

Both	**Neither**
Both Mary **and** Ann are basketball fans. **Both (of) the women** can ski. **Both women** are single. **Both of them** speak French. **Both** live in London. / They **both** live in London.	**Neither** Mary **nor** Ann likes football. **Neither of the women** can skate. **Neither woman** is married. **Neither of them** can speak German. **Neither** lives in Liverpool.

All three, all four, all five, all ...
Mary, Ann and Betty often go to the disco. **All three** women enjoy dancing. They've got a cat, a dog, a canary and a mouse. **All four** animals live happily together.

The words **both** and **neither** always refer to only two people or things. The word **all** always refers to three or more people or things: we sometimes specify the number, but not always: **all [three] of them**.

5 *Fill in* both (of), neither (of), all, none *or* some (of).

1 Russia beat Italy, but they .... *both* .... played very well.

2 Italy and Germany lost in the semi-finals. .... went into the finals.

3 Russia scored one goal, but Italy scored .... The result was 1:0.

4 Vasili, Vladimir and Mikhail come from Moscow. .... three men play for the Russian team.

5 Two Italian footballers were hurt. .... them were taken to hospital.

6 John Rivers, the English player, will spend .... his money on a good holiday. He'll save the rest for a new car.

7 John Rivers and Jerry Peters don't go skiing. .... them likes skiing.

8 How much cake have we got? — There is .... left. We ate it all while we were watching the game.

6 *Circle and correct the mistakes in the sentences below.*

1 Maria, Eleni and Anna come from Greece. (Both) of them speak Greek.

   Maria, Eleni and Anna come from Greece. All of them speak Greek.

2 If she didn't like animals, she wouldn't keep the all four dogs.

   ....

3 They don't study much, so both of them will pass the exam.

   ....

4 All we go to the same school.

   ....

5 Tina and Rosa are Italian. Two of them were born in Rome.

   ....

6 Sue and I are two going to Spain, but neither we can speak Spanish.

   ....

7 **About you**

Ask the questions below and find out what the other students do in their spare time. Then write down the results of the class survey. Use **all of us, both girls and boys, almost all, all the girls,** *etc.*

	Boys	Girls

1 Do you play football?

2 What sport do you like best, tennis or basketball?

3 Do you read a newspaper every day?

4 Do you prefer techno to rock music?

5 Do you prefer comics to books?

6 Do you help your mother with the housework?

1 All of the boys in my class play football but none of the girls do.

2 ....

3 ....

4 ....

5 ....

6 ....

29 *have something done*

They've had some things done to the house

MRS SMITH: Which is the Bakers' house?
MRS BROWN: That one with the blue door.
MRS SMITH: I didn't recognise it.
MRS BROWN: Well, they won some money on the
               lottery last month, so they've had
               some things done to the house.
MRS SMITH: Yes, I can see. They've obviously
               had a new roof fitted.
MRS BROWN: Yes, and last week they had the
               house painted outside. And they're
               going to have a new garage built too.
MRS SMITH: I'd like to win the lottery. I'd have
               my house pulled down and rebuilt!

Causative: *have something done*

Affirmative	Negative
I **have** my hair **cut** once a month.	She **doesn't have** her hair **done** very often.
We **had** our house **painted** last year.	They **didn't have** their house **decorated** last year.
She **has just had** her car **serviced** at the garage.	He **hasn't had** his car **serviced**. He's just done it himself.
I **am going to have** my watch **mended** next week.	I'm **not going to have** my bike **mended**. I'll do it myself.

1 We use the causative **have + object + past participle** construction to show that
  we are 'causing' someone else to do something for us:
  I have my hair done, cut or styled once a month. (= A hairdresser does my
  hair, cuts it or styles it: I don't do it myself.)

2 NOTE: In the simple present and simple past negatives we use **doesn't have /
  don't have** and **didn't have** (NOT 'hasn't / haven't / hadn't')

1 *Look at the text. Read these sentences and fill in the blanks.*

1 Mrs Smith didn't recognise the Bakers' house because they
  .....*have had*..... some things ....*done*......... to it.

2 They .... a new roof ....

3 They .... the house .... outside last week.

4 If Mrs Smith won the lottery, she .... her house

  .... and .... !

2 Make sentences. Put the words in the correct order.

1 her hair / Liz / cut / a year / twice / has
   Liz has her hair cut twice a year.

2 soon / have / mended / should / Mum / her shoes

   ....

3 his car / serviced / Dad / tomorrow / to have / is going

   ....

4 enough money / decorated / If I / would / I / had / my room / have

   ....

5 painted / We're / our house / have / going to

   ....

3 Complete the sentences with an appropriate past participle.

1 Liz's walkman isn't working. She must have it *repaired / mended* .

2 The house hasn't been decorated for ages. We should have all the

   rooms ....

3 Dad's watch is broken. He must have it ....

4 The car isn't running well. Dad ought to have it ....

5 Our garage is so old we should have it ....

   and then have a new one ....

Interrogative	Short answers	
	Affirmative	**Negative**
Can I have this film developed here?	Yes, you can.	No, you can't.
Did John have his photo taken?	Yes, he did.	No, he didn't.
Are they going to have their car serviced?	Yes, they are.	No, they aren't.

4 Look at the text again. Write short answers to the questions.

1 Did the Bakers have their house rebuilt?   No, they didn't.

2 Did they have a new roof fitted?   ....

3 Are they having a new garage built?   ....

4 Did they have the house painted *inside*?   ....

5 Have they had a lot of things done?   ....

5 *Who did it? Answer the question after each sentence.*

1 Mum and Dad had the kitchen painted. Who painted the kitchen — Mum and Dad or a decorator? <u>A decorator.</u>.........

2 Jane had her hair cut. Who cut Jane's hair — Jane or a hairdresser?

....

3 Jason is going to have his watch mended. Who is going to mend his watch — Jason or a watchmaker? ....

4 Mike is repairing his bike today. Who is repairing his bike — Mike or a mechanic? ....

5 Mum and Dad often have the car serviced. Who services the car — Mum and Dad or a mechanic? ....

6 *Make questions about John and his bike.*
Put the phrase **have his bike repaired** *in the correct tense.*
The answer will often help you choose the correct tense.

1 When <u>did John have his bike repaired</u> ?   Yesterday.

2 How often .... ?   Twice a year.

3 When .... ?   Tomorrow.

4 .... just .... ?   Yes, he has.

5 ....

last week if he had had enough money?   Yes, he would.

6 Where ....   At the bike shop

today?   on the corner.

7 *First make questions using the words given.*

1 When / you / last / have a tooth taken out?

   When did you last have a tooth taken out?

2 How often / you / have your house decorated?

   ....

3 When / you / next / have your eyes tested?

   ....

4 When / your parents / last / have something repaired?

   ....

5 When / you / last / have a film developed?

   ....

Now ask a friend the questions you wrote.
Write sentences about your friend.

   6 George last had a tooth taken out two weeks ago.

   7 ....

   8 ....

   9 ....

   10 ....

8 **About you**

Complete these sentences about yourself, your family or friends with any
have something done *expressions in the correct form. If you want to, you can*
use some of the expressions from the box below.

1 Even if I won some money in the lottery, I wouldn't. have my ears pierced

2 Last year at home we ....

3 I often ....

4 Perhaps next year I ....

5 Next week my best friend is going to ....

6 I've never ....

---

have [my] hair cut   have [my] room decorated   have [my] bike mended
        have [my] walkman repaired   have [my] shoes heeled
have [my] photo taken   have [my] hair dyed   have [my] ears pierced ✔

---

30 would rather (not) do, had better (not) do

I'd rather go on holiday to Greece

DAD: We've got £5,000 left from our win on the lottery! What shall we do with the money?

MUM: Let's spend some of it on a new electric cooker.

JANE: Oh, Mum, that's boring. I'd rather go on holiday to Greece. Wouldn't you, Liz?

LIZ: Yes, I would. We could visit Eleni ...

JOHN: I'd rather go to Australia. Everyone speaks English there.

MUM: John, you'd better be realistic. £5,000 isn't enough for us all to go to Australia. We'd better have a cooker.

DAD: I'm sorry, I agree with Jane and Liz. We've worked hard all year. Let's spend the money on a good holiday. And don't worry, John. Most schoolchildren in Greece speak good English anyway!

Dad, how fantastic!

would rather + (not) do	had better + (not) do
Mum **would rather buy** a new cooker. **They'd rather not fly** to Rome. **Would you rather come** with us or stay at home?	We **had better save** some money for our holiday. **You'd better not tell** him about it. **Hadn't you better stay** at home? You look very tired.

1 Both structures, **would rather** (for preferences) and **had better** (for advice), refer to the present or future, and are followed by the bare infinitive: **I would rather wait, you had better wait**.

2 We use the short form 'd in each, BUT **I'd rather = I would rather**, and **you'd better = you had better**.

3 Note the negatives **I'd rather not wait** and **you'd better not wait**, and questions **Would you rather wait ...?** and **Hadn't you better wait ...?**

1 *Answer these questions about the text in complete sentences.*

1 Mum would rather spend the money on a holiday, wouldn't she?
   No, she'd rather spend it on a new electric cooker.

2 Jane and Liz would rather visit their uncle in the USA, wouldn't they?

   ....

3 John would rather go to France, wouldn't he?

   ....

4 Dad would rather buy a new car, wouldn't he?

   ....

2 *Write what ′d stands for,* **had** *or* **would,** *in these sentences.*

1 We'd better spend the money on a new cooker.   (...had...)

2 He'd rather walk to work.   (..............)

3 He'd better see a doctor if he doesn't feel well.   (..............)

4 You'd better give him the book back.   (..............)

5 I'd rather not eat anything tonight.   (..............)

6 They'd rather spend Christmas in Australia   (..............)

7 They'd better be ready early.   (..............)

8 I think she'd rather go to university than get a job.   (..............)

3 *Rewrite these sentences using* **had better** *in the affirmative, negative or interrogative.*

1 Don't take Jane's bike without telling her.
   You'd better not take Jane's bike without telling her.

2 You should see a dentist if you have toothache.

   ....

3 Shouldn't you save this money for your summer holiday?

   ....

4 Tidy your room before mother comes back.

   ....

5 Don't lie to your mother.

   ....

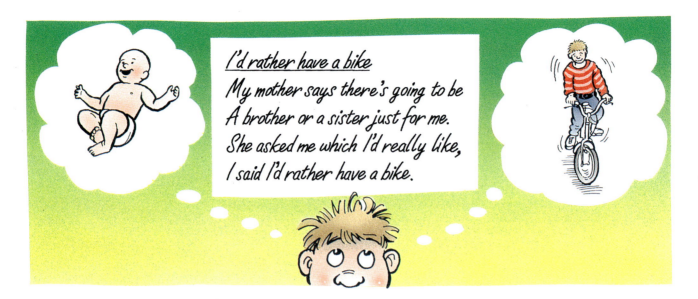

I'd rather have a bike
My mother says there's going to be
A brother or a sister just for me.
She asked me which I'd really like,
I said I'd rather have a bike.

Reporting *would rather* and *had better*

Would you like a brother or a sister?	I'**d rather have** a bike.
What did the boy say?	He **said (that) he'd rather have** a bike.
Would you rather stay here?	She **asked if I'd rather stay** there.
Shall we watch the late-night movie?	We'**d better not**.
What did she say?	**She said (that) we'd better not.**

The phrases **would rather (not)** and **had better (not)** do not change in reported speech, even when the reporting verb is in the past.

4 *Report the following sentences. Use the full forms* **would rather** *or* **had better**.

1 'I'd rather watch the football game.'

John said *he would rather watch the football game.*

2 'We'd better save our money for our holiday in Greece.'

Dad said ....

3 'Would you rather have a hamburger?'

She asked me ....

4 'You'd better not forget it.'

He told us ....

5 'Would you rather have dinner in a restaurant?'

He asked her ....

6 'Would the boys rather stay at home?'

She wanted to know ....

5 *These people want to have something done.*
Complete the sentences using the causative form.

1 Dad's car has broken down, but he can't repair it himself.

He'd better *have it repaired.* ....

2 They don't like their living room, but they don't want to decorate it themselves.

They'd rather ....

3 Our roof is damaged, but we can't fix it ourselves.

We'd better ....

4 He can't see very well, but he can't test his eyes himself.

He'd better ....

5 My hair is too long but I can't cut it very well myself.

I'd rather ....

6 About you

People ask your advice about presents for your family and friends.
Advise them using **would rather** *and* **had better**.

1 Somebody wants to send your father a science fiction book.

I think my father would rather have a book of detective stories. ....
I think you'd better get him a book by Agatha Christie. ....

2 Your father wants to give your mother a bike for her birthday.

....

....

3 Your uncle wants to send some comic books to your grandfather.

....

....

4 Somebody wants to buy your friend a pet snake.

....

....

5 Somebody suggests that you give your friend a dictionary as a birthday present.

....

....

Irregular verbs

Base form	Simple past	Past participle	Base form	Simple past	Past participle
be	was / were	been	let	let	let
bear	bore	born	lie	lay	lain
beat	beat	beaten	lose	lost	lost
become	became	become	make	made	made
begin	began	begun	meet	met	met
blow	blew	blown	pay	paid	paid
break	broke	broken	put	put	put
bring	brought	brought	read	read	read
build	built	built	ride	rode	ridden
buy	bought	bought	ring	rang	rung
catch	caught	caught	run	ran	run
choose	chose	chosen	say	said	said
come	came	come	see	saw	seen
cost	cost	cost	sell	sold	sold
cut	cut	cut	send	sent	sent
dig	dug	dug	set (out)	set (out)	set (out)
do	did	done	sing	sang	sung
dream	dreamt / dreamed	dreamt / dreamed	sink	sank	sunk
			sit	sat	sat
drink	drank	drunk	sleep	slept	slept
drive	drove	driven	smell	smelt / smelled	smelt / smelled
eat	ate	eaten			
fall	fell	fallen	speak	spoke	spoken
feel	felt	felt	spend	spent	spent
fight	fought	fought	spill	spilt / spilled	spilt / spilled
find	found	found	stand	stood	stood
fly	flew	flown	steal	stole	stolen
forget	forgot	forgotten	sting	stung	stung
get	got	got	sweep	swept	swept
give	gave	given	swim	swam	swum
go	went	gone	take	took	taken
grow	grew	grown	teach	taught	taught
have	had	had	tell	told	told
hear	heard	heard	think	thought	thought
hide	hid	hidden	throw	threw	thrown
hold	held	held	understand	understood	understood
hurt	hurt	hurt	wake (up)	woke (up)	woken (up)
keep	kept	kept	wear	wore	worn
know	knew	known	win	won	won
learn	learnt / learned	learnt / learned	write	wrote	written
leave	left	left			